MW01357594

BIRDING GUIDE
to the
Denver-Boulder Region

by Robert Folzenlogen

Pruett Publishing / Boulder / 1986

*Dedicated to the memory of
Gilbert Siegel, my grandfather,
who instilled in me a fascination
with wild creatures.*

©1986 By Bob Folzenlogen

First Edition

1 2 3 4 5 6 7 8 9

Library of Congress Cataloging-in-Publication Data

Folzenlogen, Bob, 1950-
    Birding guide to the Denver-Boulder region.

    Bibliography: p.
    Includes index.
    1. Bird watching—Colorado—Denver Region. 2. Bird
watching—Colorado—Boulder Region. I. Title
QL684.C6F65   1986   598'.07'23478883   86-4969
ISBN 0-87108-710-3 (pbk.)

Printed in the United States of America

Contents

Birds of the Region /61

Foreword

Since my early childhood days, when I watched my grandfather feed the birds and squirrels in his backyard, I have been fascinated by wildlife and the natural environment. However, it was not until I moved to the North Carolina coast, at the age of twenty-five, that I began to take a more careful look at our environment and at the myriad of creatures in it. It was then that I became a devoted birder and began to keep my "life list." I soon realized that the pleasure of birding came just as much from hiking through wild areas as it did from "hunting" for new birds. I also began to appreciate the fact that birding expands one's awareness of wild plants and animals that might otherwise go unnoticed.

As I moved from one city to another, it would usually take several months to learn where the best birding spots were and where to find certain birds. Though local birding lists and Audubon newsletters were helpful, I could never find a publication that condensed and organized this information.

I have thus decided to produce this book, as a resource for birders moving to the Denver-Boulder area or visiting our region, and as a guide for beginning birders. It is not a scientific study of the birdlife in our region but does represent a composite of my observations over the past few years. It is not intended to replace the standard field guides but, rather, to be used in concert with those texts. This book is not proposed to be complete in any way; however, I have attempted to represent all birds that are at least fairly common in our region and have chosen the birding areas with the goal of covering the various habitat types found in eastern and central Colorado.

The text has been divided into three sections. The first, "Birding Areas of the Denver-Boulder Region," describes fifteen areas that are accessible to the public throughout the year. For twelve of these areas, maps are included to illustrate the specific locations mentioned in the text. I have attempted to summarize the primary features of each area, with emphasis on the local bird population and its variability throughout the year.

The second section lists the birds themselves, arranged and grouped to correspond with the major field guides. For each bird, the following facts are listed: dates in area, local habitat, breeding and wintering grounds, comments regarding its behavior and a recommended time and place for finding that bird.

The third section lists suggested field trips through the year, designed to capsulize information from the first two sections and to guide the birder through the seasons, directing him/her to birding highlights and encouraging exposure to a wide variety of habitats.

It is my sincere hope that this text will serve not only as a useful guide to the birds of the Denver-Boulder region but also as a vehicle for increasing the reader's awareness of the natural preserves within our area and for prompting a greater devotion to protecting such open spaces throughout our state, our country and our planet.

Robert Folzenlogen

Magpie.

Birding Areas of the Region

This section of the text discusses fifteen areas within our region that provide excellent birding throughout the year. There are certainly many other good birding spots along the Front Range, and some favorite haunts may not be included.

The areas have been selected on the basis of their accessibility to the public and the bird habitats they offer. I have attempted to choose areas that are distributed throughout the various life zones that characterize the general Front Range environment, from plains to tundra. Some duplication is inevitable but each area is unique in its setting and each will provide an enjoyable birding experience during any season of the year.

I have specifically chosen to exclude urban parks, since wildlife in these areas has generally become unnaturally tolerant of, if not dependent upon, human activity. On the other hand, many of these parks, such as Sloan Lake and Washington Park, in Denver, afford an excellent opportunity to study certain birds, especially waterfowl, at close range. In addition, these areas are great for introducing young children to the joy of watching wildlife.

To fully appreciate each area, I strongly recommend that you visit during each season of the year. In addition, it is important to realize that birds tend to be most active, and thus most visible, during the early morning and late afternoon hours. Some birds, such as most owls, night herons, poor-wills and rails, are best seen at dusk. Regardless of when and where you go, knowing what to look for will add to your success and enjoyment. Hopefully, this text will prove helpful in that respect.

KEY TO THE MAPS

Roads: ————————————

Parking Areas:

Trails: - - - - - - - - - - - - -

Lakes, Streams:

Marshes:

Trees, Thickets:

Barr Lake State Park

THE
PLAINS

Barr Lake is a large reservoir in Adams County, approximately 18 miles northeast of Denver. The lake and surrounding 550 acres of land are part of the Colorado State Park system.

To birders and naturalists this park is perhaps best known for its breeding population of western grebes and for the large number of white pelicans that gather here during the summer months. Though the local ecology is limited to grassland, lake and marsh habitats, Barr Lake is renowned for its tremendous diversity of birdlife.

The southern half of the park has been preserved as a wildlife sanctuary. A "nature area" parking lot is located near the southeastern end of the reservoir, and from there a trail winds along the adjacent shores of the lake. This trail parallels the route of the diversion canal (see map) but side-trails lead down to boardwalks and duck blinds extending over the water. One of these side-trails leads over an elevated boardwalk to a gazebo on a small island near the southwestern end of the reservoir. From the gazebo one has an excellent view of the heronry hugging the lake's western shore.

Early May is an excellent time to visit Barr Lake. Most of the summer residents have arrived, spring migrations are still underway and the mosquito hordes have not yet materialized. In the thickets along the lake white-crowned sparrows, yellow-rumped warblers, chipping sparrows and house wrens are usually abundant. Swainson's and hermit thrushes, Bullock's orioles and western wood pewees are also found in these moist woodlands. Barn and tree swallows swoop along the canal and skim the lake waters, filling their bellies with insects.

On the grasslands kestrels, northern harriers and Swainson's hawks will be found. Western meadowlarks, magpies, horned larks and mourning doves are also common on the prairie.

Water birds tend to congregate along the southern rim of the reservoir, especially near the inlet stream. In early May blue-winged teal, cinnamon teal and northern shovelers are very common, feeding with mallards, pintail and coot in the shallow marshes. Wilson's phalaropes often stop by in huge flocks. Killdeer and spotted sandpipers forage along the lakeshore as red-winged and yellow-headed blackbirds move about the marsh.

Out on the reservoir the western grebes have paired off and, if you're lucky, you can witness their famous mating dance. Double-crested cormorants and great blue herons are nesting in the rookery and white pelicans, still few in number, fish on the lake. White-faced ibis and cattle egrets occasionally stop by in May, but their presence is unpredictable.

Returning to Barr Lake in August, the visitor will find that the water level has fallen and that large mudflats are appearing along the shorelines. Unfortunately, the mosquito population has exploded and insect repellent is a must. Undeterred by these "pests" and, indeed, benefitting from their presence, songbirds are abundant along the reservoir. House wrens, orioles and yellowthroats are the most conspicuous. Yellow warblers, black-capped chickadees and warbling vireos are also found. Eastern and western kingbirds, gathering in larger flocks as the days shorten, flycatch from the drowned cottonwood trees. Red-headed woodpeckers, favoring wooded marshes, are fairly common, especially along the eastern shore. Blue grosbeaks are easily found at Barr during the summer months; males often sing from the small trees that line the canal. Loggerhead shrikes, fairly common from April to October, are usually seen on the grasslands, hunting from fenceposts.

On the lake western grebes will be found with young in tow. White pelicans, peaking in numbers, often glide high overhead on these late-summer afternoons. In the heronry snowy egrets have joined the cormorants and great blue herons.

Winter at Barr Lake.

Black-crowned night herons, which also roost here, are often found feeding along the marsh.

The fall shorebird migration is well underway by August. The growing mudflats attract marbled godwits, long-billed curlews, stilt sandpipers and semipalmated plovers. Western and pectoral sandpipers are also among the early migrants. As the season progresses the reservoir continues to shrink, mudflats expand and shorebirds increase in number and variety, peaking in early September. In addition to the shorebird waves, late summer brings large flocks of California and Franklin's gulls to the Barr Lake area. These gulls, having nested on the surrounding prairies, stop by to rest and feed before heading south. Small flocks of black and Forster's terns also pass through in August and September.

By late October the reservoir resembles a shallow river. On the deeper pools migrating loons, grebes and waterfowl congregate in large, mixed flocks. Vast numbers of Canada geese feed on the exposed lake bed. Along the rim of the shrinking reservoir, large flocks of yellowlegs, long-billed dowitchers, shovelers and green-winged teal gather

BARR LAKE
1. *Main Entrance*
2. *Heronry*
3. *Gazebo*
4. *Nature Area Parking*
5. *Inlet Area*
6. *Diversion Canal*

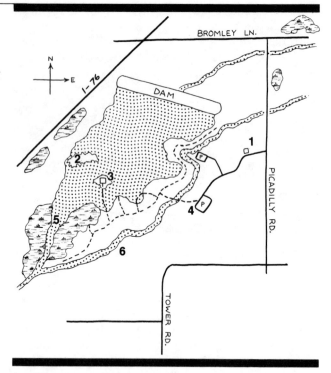

in the shallow waters. Sandhill cranes, migrating through from late September through mid-November, occasionally stop by in sizable flocks.

In the thickets dark-eyed juncos, black-capped chickadees and tree sparrows now predominate. Ring-necked pheasants are conspicuous on the grassland, wary of the red-tailed and ferruginous hawks circling overhead.

Returning in winter the visitor will find that the lake is frozen over and covered with snow. But even in this seemingly bleak environment, birders will not be disappointed. Horned larks, magpies, pheasants and, less reliably, longspurs feed on the grasslands. Rough-legged hawks, down from the Arctic, replace the Swainson's hawks that have headed to South America. Along the frozen reservoir dark-eyed juncos, black-capped chickadees and tree sparrows forage among the thickets. On occasion they are joined by flocks of common redpolls that wander down from Canada. Downy woodpeckers and northern flickers are common in the woodlands. Screech and great horned owls, more conspicuous now on the bare limbs, roost in cottonwood trees. Long-eared and short-eared owls, uncommon visitors during the winter months, may also be found.

Be sure to stop by the inlet area during your winter visit. Open water often persists here, attracting the ducks and geese that remain through the colder months. In addition, bald eagles are often found resting in the trees along the stream.

The countryside that surrounds Barr Lake State Park offers additional birding opportunities. The local prairie and farmland is studded with potholes and sloughs that fill with water each spring, attracting migrants such as teal, phalaropes and shorebirds. Check the prairie marshes for bitterns, soras, Virginia rails and coot during the warmer months. The open grasslands along Tower Road attract lark sparrows and lark buntings during the summer and occasional flocks of longspurs during the colder months.

In addition to the excellent diversity of birds, the Barr Lake area abounds with other wildlife. White-tailed and mule deer are both found here. Red fox are especially common. On spring evenings the visitor may encounter a litter of fox cubs playing near their den.

To reach Barr Lake from Denver, take I-25 ★ north and exit onto I-76 toward Ft. Morgan. After driving for approximately 15 miles along I-76, you will see the reservoir east of the highway. Drive two miles further and turn right (east) on Bromley Lane. Drive for almost one mile and turn right (south) on Picadilly Road, which will take you to the park entrance (see map). At the time of this writing, the entrance fee is $3.00 per vehicle.

Chatfield Reservoir

Chatfield Reservoir is a 1150 acre lake, created by a dam at the confluence of Plum Creek and the South Platte River, approximately eight miles southwest of Denver. It was constructed in the late 1960's, primarily for flood control.

Today, the Reservoir and surrounding 5600 acres of land are part of the Colorado State Park system. The Chatfield Recreation Area is a favorite spot for fishing, boating, horseback riding, bicycling and hot-air ballooning. The area also provides a tremendous diversity of habitats for birds and other wildlife. From the birder's point of view, the reservoir is best known for the heronry near its southern shore. During the warmer months great blue herons and double-crested cormorants nest here in large numbers.

It is helpful to look at Chatfield as four overlapping areas:

1. *The Lake.* The reservoir itself abounds with water birds throughout most of the year. Ducks peak in number and variety each April and October. American coot, pied-billed grebes and the surface-feeding ducks (such as widgeon, gadwalls, shovelers and pintail) favor the shallow waters and tend to congregate near the southwestern end of the lake. Western grebes, Canada geese, redheads, lesser scaup and buffleheads form large rafts out on the deeper waters.

A trail along the southern shore of the reservoir offers good birding throughout the year but especially in mid-May. At this time of year migrant songbirds fill the trees and thickets that border the lake. Look for western tanagers, Bullock's orioles, yellow warblers and various flycatchers. Barn and tree swallows swoop above the lake, feasting on the growing hordes of insects. Along the marshy beaver ponds that dot the shoreline, look for American bitterns and soras feeding among the cattails. Out in the heronry great blue herons and double-crested cormorants tend to their noisy fledglings as ring-billed gulls wait below, ready to retrieve any morsels of food that drop from the nests. Ospreys, which often stop by to rest and fish here, are best found during their migrations, in late April and early October.

At the mouth of Plum Creek, near the eastern end of the reservoir, large mudflats have formed from the silt carried by the stream. During late summer and especially during dry springs, hundreds of shorebirds may gather here as they migrate through our region. In early May look for avocets, stilt sandpipers, black-bellied plovers and semi-

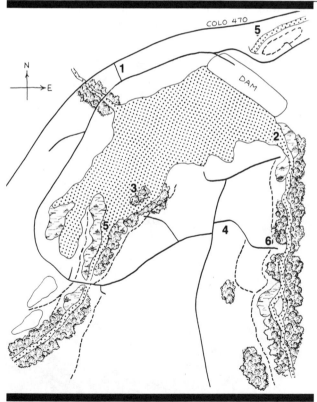

CHATFIELD RESERVOIR
1. *Main Entrance*
2. *Plum Creek Inlet*
3. *Heronry*
4. *Prairie Dog Town*
5. *South Platte River*
6. *Nature Area*

palmated sandpipers. Killdeer are common here throughout the warmer months. The fall migration begins by late July and generally peaks in early September. Yellowlegs, long-billed dowitchers and Baird's sandpipers are among the more common fall visitors.

During the winter the reservoir is relatively devoid of birds. Flocks of Canada geese return to rest here, spending much of their day feeding on adjacent fields and grasslands. Ring-billed gulls, occasionally joined by herring gulls, gather along the open water. If open water remains, mergansers, goldeneyes and buffleheads will stay through the winter.

2. *The Grasslands.* An expansive scrub-prairie surrounds the reservoir, especially along its southern flank. A network of trails provides access, though most of the grassland residents are readily

Plum Creek Inlet.

seen from the road. During the warmer months western meadowlarks and mourning doves are abundant here. Grassland sparrows (vesper, lark, savannah) are often found along the trails. Ring-necked pheasants, present throughout the year, are most easily seen from late fall through early spring, when the prairie grasses are thinned and compressed by snow. Magpies, kestrels and red-tailed hawks patrol the grasslands throughout the year, joined by Swainson's hawks in the summer and rough-legged hawks in the winter. Northern harriers also hunt on the prairie and are most common in spring and fall. During the colder months flocks of horned larks, occasionally joined by longspurs, roam across the prairie.

A prairie dog town is located along the road to the Nature Area. In addition to the entertainment provided by these social creatures a visit to this area offers a good chance to see burrowing owls, especially from May through October. These ground nesters are often seen standing atop old prairie dog mounds, patiently scouting for grass-hoppers.

3. *The Feeder Streams.* In addition to the lake itself, the reservoir dam has formed a series of marshes, backwater swamps and flooded woodlands along the course of the feeder streams. Trails meander southward from the reservoir, skirting the marshes and crossing into the cottonwood groves. This moist habitat attracts an excellent diversity of birds and other wildlife. Mallards and wood ducks nest in the marshes and are often seen with young in tow during the summer months. Blue-winged, cinnamon and green-winged teal are also attracted to these backwaters and are most abundant during spring migration. Belted kingfishers patrol the waterways and are often seen resting on limbs that overhang the stream. Great horned owls are common in the wooded swamps, enduring harrass-ment from the eastern kingbirds and magpies also nesting here. During the warmer months house wrens, American goldfinches, yellowthroats and

yellow warblers are usually abundant in the moist thickets. Song sparrows are common along the streams throughout the year.

With the approach of winter, the summer songbirds depart for the south. In their place dark-eyed juncos, tree sparrows, chickadees and nut-hatches forage among the cottonwoods. Northern flickers and downy woodpeckers, present yearlong, are occasionally joined by flocks of Lewis' wood-peckers moving down from the foothill forests.

4. *The Lower South Platte.* Below the dam the South Platte River renews itself and flows onward toward Metro Denver. During much of the year the waters are shallow, attracting great blue herons and black-crowned night herons to feed along the shores. Killdeer and spotted sandpipers forage along the sandbars during the warmer months. Belted kingfishers are common here throughout the year.

During the colder months the open waters of the river attract the local winter ducks, such as mallards, common mergansers and buffleheads. Tree sparrows are often abundant in the thickets that line the shore and northern shrikes occasionally hunt from the small trees that dot the adjacent grasslands.

In addition to the excellent birding, Chatfield provides a diverse environment that offers food and shelter for many other wild creatures. These include mule deer, beavers, muskrats, red foxes, prairie dogs and many other small mammals. Thirteen-lined ground squirrels are especially conspicuous as they dash across the roadways during the summer months. As you hike along the trails, watch for bull snakes and rattlesnakes that leave the tall grass to sun themselves in the open areas.

★ To reach Chatfield from Denver, head south on I-25, University Avenue, Broadway or Sante Fe, to Colorado Route 470 (County Line Road). Take 470 west to the Reservoir, which lies near the base of the foothills. At the time of this writing, the entrance fee is $3.00 per vehicle.

Cherry Creek Reservoir

Cherry Creek Recreation Area is part of the Colorado State Park system. It is a well-known and heavily used area, centered around an 880-acre reservoir. Most of the human activity is concentrated on and around the lake and at the picnic and camping grounds. The park is popular for swimming, sailing, fishing, bicycling and cross-country skiing.

Cherry Creek Reservoir is also an excellent spot for birding. A "nature area" has been established at the southeast end of the lake in a marsh and grassland habitat. A trail meanders in and out of the marsh, elevated by boardwalks at high-water points. Another trail winds along the southern shore of the reservoir, angling out across the adjacent grassland. A third trail follows Cherry Creek south and east from the parking area.

On a spring morning there is much to see here. Meadowlarks, magpies and mourning doves are common on the grassland. Ring-necked pheasants, abundant due to lack of hunting pressure, often cross one's path. In the trees and thickets that border the marsh, house wrens and American goldfinches are easily found. Northern harriers are especially common in April and May, often seen perched above the marsh's southern border. Swainson's hawks, returning from their winter in South America, soar high above the grasslands.

Out on the reservoir migrating waterfowl cluster near the eastern shore. Northern shovelers, blue-winged teal, coot and American widgeon are usually most abundant. Western and horned grebes feed on the deeper waters, while their pied-billed cousins favor the shallow lake margins. By early May white pelicans, snowy egrets and white-faced ibis occasionally stop by on their way to northern breeding grounds. Canada geese and mallards, many of which have wintered here, have paired off and are beginning to nest along the marsh. Magpies can be seen gathering twigs for their huge

CHERRY CREEK
RESERVOIR
1. *West Gate*
2. *Northeast Inlet*
3. *East Gate*
4. *Nature Area*
5. *Prairie Dog Town*

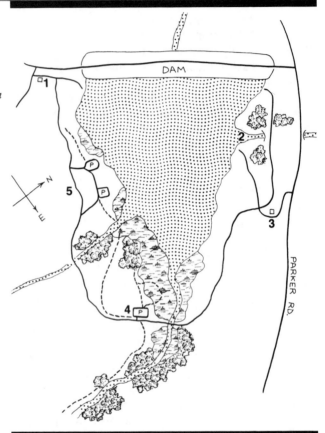

nests; in later years many of these nests will be
used by great horned owls.

Hiking along Cherry Creek, the visitor will
likely encounter newly arrived willets, spotted
sandpipers, killdeer and other shorebirds. Common
snipe are often found in the marshy pools that
border the creek.

Returning on a mid-summer evening, the birder
will find yellowthroats, house finches, lazuli
buntings and American goldfinches bustling about
the marsh thickets. Great blue herons and black-
crowned night herons feed along the shallows, and

the patient birder may spot a Virginia rail or sora as it slips through the marsh. Though the bird itself is rarely seen, the unmistakable call of the American bittern is often heard. During the evening hours huge flocks of robins, blackbirds, magpies and ring-billed gulls return to the area to roost, having spent the day feeding in the surrounding countryside. As the sun sets behind the Front Range, the familiar hoot of the great horned owl rises from the marsh. These nocturnal hunters can usually be seen at dusk, silently departing the woodlands to feed on the nearby prairie.

Fall migrants begin to appear by August. Shorebirds gather on exposed sandbars and mudflats. Waterfowl, led by blue-winged and cinnamon teal, gradually increase in number and variety, peaking by late October. In mid-September the shrubs and thickets begin to fill with migrant songbirds, including warbling vireos, yellow-rumped warblers and white-crowned sparrows. Ospreys often stop by to fish on the reservoir, especially in early October.

November is a good time to visit Cherry Creek Reservoir. Cold northern winds have brought fresh recruits down from their Canadian breeding grounds. These include common loons, goldeneyes, common and hooded mergansers and buffleheads. They join the flocks of Canada geese and western grebes that have been building through the fall. Ring-billed gulls, always common here, begin to increase in number as winter approaches.

Along the marsh, song and tree sparrows are settling in for the colder months. Flocks of Brewer's blackbirds mingle with the redwings that still dominate the marsh. Out on the grassland horned larks are increasing in numbers and ring-necked pheasants, energized by the autumn chill, are even more conspicuous.

Natural areas are not truly appreciated unless they are visited in all seasons. A trip to Cherry Creek Reservoir on a sunny winter day, free from the summer crowds and buzzing mosquitos, is always a pleasant experience. Winter has silenced the insects and tree frogs and snow dampens your footsteps. But nature's cycle has not shut down. Flocks of geese move about the area and, if open water remains, mergansers, goldeneyes and buffleheads feed on the reservoir. Pheasants and magpies still forage on the grasslands. Kestrels, red-tailed hawks and great horned owls continue their predations, joined by rough-legged hawks and northern shrikes down from Canada. Juncos, nuthatches and black-capped chickadees hunt for seeds in the winter marsh.

Near the northern end of the reservoir, a feeder stream enters from the east (see map). This stream travels underground for several hundred yards and is warmed by the earth. The resulting open waters attract common snipe, mallards and other birds that have stayed for the winter.

In addition to the abundant birdlife, Cherry Creek Recreation Area provides a home for many

Along Cherry Creek, late summer.

of the eastern-plains mammals, such as white-tailed deer, beavers, muskrats, skunks, jackrabbits and ground squirrels. A prairie dog town is located south of the reservoir (see map).

To reach the Cherry Creek Recreation Area ★ from Denver, take I-25 south to I-225. Head east on I-225 (toward Aurora) and take the Parker Road exit. Turn right on Parker Road and either proceed directly to the east entrance or cross the dam to the west gate. At the time of this writing, the entrance fee is $3.00 per vehicle. During the summer months plan to visit on a weekday, since weekend crowds are usually large.

McClellan Reservoir & The Highline Canal

McClellan is a relatively small reservoir near the intersection of County Line Road and Santa Fe (U.S. 85), in southwestern Metro Denver. Though there is no public access to the lake, several pull-offs along County Line Road and a trail along the adjacent Highline Canal, provide the birder with vantage points from which to view the reservoir. I consider McClellan to be the best spot in our region for observing most of the bay (diving) ducks.

During the summer months few water birds are found on the reservoir. Usually a pair or two of wood ducks nest in the marsh at the eastern end of the lake. Mallards and Canada geese also nest here in small numbers. Double-crested cormorants fish on the reservoir but usually return to the Chatfield heronry to roost and nest. Likewise, great blue herons feed along the shores, but are just visitors here, nesting elsewhere.

While the lake itself is fairly quiet during the summer, the grasslands, marshes and woodlands that surround it are experiencing the peak of their yearly life cycles. This is a good time to do some

birding along the Highline Canal, which winds
around the southern and eastern flanks of the reservoir. This canal, constructed to bring irrigation
waters to the eastern plains, originates in Waterton
Canyon. It then snakes its way for over seventy
miles through the Denver and Aurora suburbs
before flowing onto the farmlands. A hiking trail
follows the canal throughout its route, offering an
avenue for exercise (and birding) across the Metro
area. The section of this trail that loops around
McClellan passes through natural areas that, to
date, remain relatively undisturbed. Nevertheless,
"development" is slowly encroaching on this area,

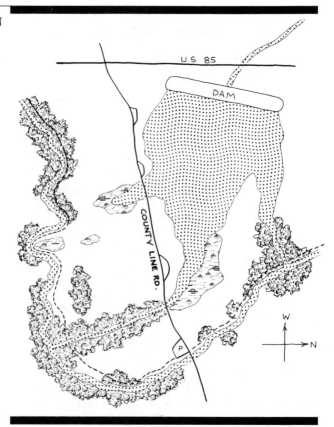

**McCLELLAN
RESERVOIR**

U.S. 85

DAM

COUNTY LINE RD.

P

W

N

and, as it does, habitats are altered and wildlife is displaced.

Following the trail south and west from the parking lot on County Line Road (see map), the visitor is treated to an excellent diversity of birdlife. The canal is lined with low thickets and tall cottonwoods. During these warmer months house wrens, rufous-sided towhees, Bullock's orioles and yellow warblers feed among the thickets. Magpies, northern flickers, house finches and downy woodpeckers are common throughout the year. Mallards and wood ducks are often found on the canal, and, in summer, usually have ducklings in tow.

On the uphill side of the canal a prairie grassland begins. Western and eastern kingbirds are common here during the warmer months, usually perched on wires, fences or old tree stumps that border the prairie. Kestrels, red-tails and Swainson's hawks may be seen as they hunt for mice and rabbits. Western meadowlarks, mourning doves and various grassland sparrows are also found in this area.

Downhill from the canal, the local environment is characterized by weedy fields, scattered thickets and small cattail marshes. Barn, tree and rough-winged swallows swoop along McClellan's feeder stream, and songbirds (warblers, vireos and flycatchers) find this moist and "buggy" habitat quite attractive. Look for western wood pewees, yellow warblers and warbling vireos here, especially where the trail dips to cross the stream. The cattail marshes fill with red-winged blackbirds during the warmer months and offer choice habitat for soras, bitterns and marsh wrens. Black-crowned night herons often feed along these ponds and are best observed at dusk or dawn.

Back on the reservoir, activity begins to increase by mid-September, as large flocks of Franklin's gulls stop by to rest. In early October pied-billed grebes, western grebes, coot and widgeon begin to gather on the lake. Later in the month they are joined by common loons, redheads and

Cottonwoods shade the Highline Canal.

ring-necked ducks that have begun their southward migration. Rarely, arctic loons may be spotted on the lake, especially in late October.

During November lesser scaup, common goldeneyes, buffleheads and common mergansers arrive from the north. They are occasionally joined by small flocks of canvasbacks and hooded mergansers. On a few occasions, always in November, I have seen peregrine falcons here. They perch on trees that border the lake and, after prolonged observation, suddenly streak across the water, hoping to grab a duck as it bolts into the air. To date, on these occasions, the ducks have managed to escape by diving underwater.

The deepest part of the reservoir usually remains open throughout the winter. From December through mid-February wintering ducks congregate on the shrinking lake surface. Common and hooded mergansers, common goldeneyes and buffleheads fish on the water while huge flocks of

ring-billed gulls gather along the ice. Small flocks
of herring gulls often join the ring-bills and are
most often seen in December.

The spring thaw usually begins by late February
and by mid-March most of the lake is free of ice.
Among the first spring migrants are the horned
grebes, still in their winter plumage. They are
joined in March by redheads, lesser scaup and ring-
necked ducks, stopping by to rest and feed before
moving on to breeding grounds in the north. By
late March ruddy ducks, coot and gadwalls appear
on the lake.

Activity on the reservoir usually peaks in mid-
April. Horned grebes have increased in number and
have taken on their breeding plumage. Western
grebes begin to appear, often in large flocks.
American widgeon, shovelers and teal (blue-winged
and green-winged) gather along the shallow lake
margins. By mid-May, most of the waterfowl have
moved on and the reservoir enters another quiet
summer season.

To reach McClellan Reservoir from Denver,   ★
head south on I-25 and take the County Line Road
exit. Head west on County Line Road until you
reach the reservoir. A small parking area for the
Highline Canal sits on the south side of the road
(see map).

Sawhill/Walden Ponds

Sawhill and Walden Ponds are adjacent wildlife
preserves in eastern Boulder County, centered
around a network of reclaimed gravel pits that lie
in the flood plain of Boulder Creek. Nature, with
man's assistance, has gradually converted the pits
back to a series of ponds and marshes, separated
by brushy clearings and groves of cottonwood trees.
Sawhill is part of the City of Boulder Open Space
system, while Walden Ponds is managed by Boulder
County. The birds and other wild creatures do not
concern themselves with such man-made distinc-

tions and, for the purposes of this discussion, the two preserves will be treated as a continuous wildlife habitat. This entire area is perhaps the best location to study the flora and fauna of the eastern Colorado marsh habitat that can be found in our region.

Arriving at dawn on a summer morning, the birder will find great blue herons, black-crowned night herons and an occasional green-backed heron feeding along the shallow marsh waters. Patient observation may uncover a sora or Virginia rail as it slips among the reeds. Killdeer and spotted sandpipers are conspicuous as they forage along the mudflats. Less obvious are the common snipe and American bitterns that favor the dense cattail swamps. Red-winged and yellow-headed blackbirds provide a noisy background chorus, as yellowthroats, song sparrows and marsh wrens chime in to greet the morning sun. Barn, tree and rough-winged swallows swoop over the ponds, feasting on the numerous insects. The groves of cottonwoods are home to northern flickers, downy woodpeckers and great horned owls. They also provide perches for the red-tailed hawks, northern harriers and kestrels, as they scan the clearings for unwary rodents. Magpies, mourning doves and meadowlarks feed in the grassy areas, while house wrens and goldfinches move about the thickets. Belted kingfishers patrol the waterways and are especially common along Boulder Creek. Canada geese, mallards and pied-billed grebes nest along the marshes and, by midsummer, are usually seen with young in tow. Eastern kingbirds, favoring this wooded marsh habitat, are common during the warmer months.

Returning in October, the visitor will find an excellent variety of waterfowl, which stop by the ponds to rest and feed as they move to wintering grounds. American widgeon and ring-necked ducks are especially common, accompanied by coot, gadwalls, pintail, redheads and green-winged teal. Canada geese are dramatically increasing in numbers, as the local residents are joined by migrants from the north. Greater white-fronted geese, though far less common, are also regular visitors and are best found in late September or early October. Killdeer and spotted sandpipers still feed along the mudflats, joined by small groups of yellowlegs and long-billed dowitchers. White-crowned sparrows and yellow-rumped warblers, having summered in the mountains, forage among the thickets before heading south. Early October is also a good time to look for ospreys, which stop by to fish on their way to southern coasts.

Summer marsh, Sawhill Ponds.

By mid-December, the ponds and marshes have usually frozen over and the waterfowl have moved on to open waters. Valmont Reservoir, just south of Sawhill Ponds, is warmed by a power plant and thus provides an oasis for the geese, ducks and other water birds that winter in the area. Back at the Ponds tree sparrows are abundant in the thickets, joining the black-capped chickadees and house finches that remain through the year. Great horned owls, kestrels and red-tailed hawks still patrol the grasslands, accompanied by rough-legged hawks and northern shrikes that have left Canada to winter in balmy Colorado. Northern flickers and downy woodpeckers, undaunted by the cold, continue to search the cottonwoods for hibernating insects, but now must compete with brown creepers and nuthatches that have descended from the mountain forests. Boulder Creek, due to its rapid flow, usually remains open and attracts the mallards and kingfishers that have not moved south.

By late February the ponds are beginning to thaw and waterfowl are returning. Among the first to arrive are the pintail and green-winged teal, favoring the shallow marsh waters. By mid-March flocks of redheads and ring-necked ducks appear on the larger ponds, soon to be joined by lesser scaup and horned grebes. Northern shovelers, widgeon, gadwalls and coot mingle along the shallow pond margins. Blue-winged and cinnamon teal begin to arrive in mid-April, joining the mallards and pied-billed grebes that haunt the marshy areas. April also brings flocks of yellow-headed blackbirds, which tend to congregate along the large, central pond at Walden. White-crowned sparrows and yellow-rumped warblers, heading back to the mountains, have replaced the tree sparrows that have departed for their breeding grounds in Canada. Swallows begin to return by mid-April and, in late May, Forster's and black terns often stop by to feast on the growing hordes of insects. Eastern kingbirds, also arriving in May, nest in the trees that border the marsh. The summer season has returned to the Ponds.

In addition to the excellent birding, a visit to this area provides an opportunity to see many other creatures that characterize our local marsh habitat. Most conspicuous are the beavers and muskrats that glide across the ponds, repairing their lodges or gathering food for their winter retreats. Bull-frogs and turtles lounge along the mudflats as garter and bull snakes wind through the marsh grass. If you stay until dusk, you may see raccoons

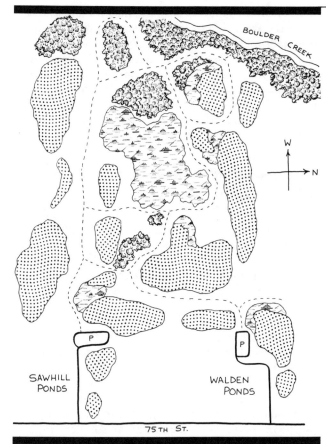

**SAWHILL PONDS/
WALDEN PONDS**

or red foxes as they emerge from their dens for a
night of hunting.

To reach Sawhill/Walden Ponds from Denver,
take I-25 north and exit onto U.S. 36, toward
Boulder. After driving for 13.5 miles along U.S.
36, take the Superior-Louisville exit. Turn right
(north) on the county road. Drive 1.7 miles and
then turn left (west) on South Boulder Road. Drive
one-half mile and turn right (north) on 76th Street.
Drive almost one mile and turn left (west) on Baseline Road. Drive one block and turn right (north)
on 75th Street. Drive approximately 2.5 miles to

the entrance roads, which lead into the preserves from the west side of 75th Street, approximately one-half mile north of the intersection with Valmont Road (see map). There is no entrance fee.

An alternative way is to continue on U.S. 36 (which becomes 28th Street) into Boulder and turn right (east) on Valmont Road. Then turn left on 75th Street and drive the half-mile to the entrance roads.

West Quincy Lakes

There are many small lakes and reservoirs scattered throughout the Denver-Boulder region that provide breeding habitat or migration rest-stops for waterfowl. Several of these lakes lie along West Quincy Avenue, in southwest Metro Denver. The following discussion will be limited to two lakes that lie across the road from one another, approximately one-half mile west of Wadsworth Boulevard. Though both are on private land, the lakes can be easily viewed from pull-offs along West Quincy Avenue.

In late February the frozen lakes begin to thaw and a new life cycle begins. By mid-March redheads, lesser scaup and gadwalls are usually abundant here. They are joined by smaller numbers of ring-necks, buffleheads and common goldeneyes. Muskrats are emerging from their winter beneath the ice, and red-winged blackbirds claim their nesting sites in the surrounding marsh. By late March American widgeons, pied-billed grebes and numerous coot appear on the lakes. Large flocks of canvasbacks may stop by as they head toward their northern breeding grounds.

Yellow-headed blackbirds usually return by mid-April, adding their distinctive calls to the constant din of the redwings. Blue-winged and cinnamon teal, also arriving in April, are best found on the shallow lake south of West Quincy Avenue.

Autumn at the Lakes.

Early May is a good time to look for Wilson's phalaropes, which occasionally stop by in huge flocks. Mallards, pied-billed grebes, coot, ruddy ducks and cinnamon teal nest in the marshes and, by early summer, are often seen with their young. During the warmer months double-crested cormorants feed on the larger lake and great blue herons often hunt along the shores.

With the cool winds of autumn, waterfowl begin to return in large numbers. Franklin's gulls may appear in large flocks during September. In early October, pied-billed grebes, gadwalls, widgeons and coot are common here. Ospreys, heading south for the winter, may stop by to fish on the larger lake. In mid-October redheads, ruddy ducks and ring-necks usually appear in sizable flocks.

By late October the winter ducks are arriving, including common goldeneyes and buffleheads. They are joined by lesser scaup, canvasbacks and increasing numbers of Canada geese. Activity on the lakes usually peaks in early November. As the days shorten and the night temperatures drop, the lakes begin to freeze over and the waterfowl disperse to open waters.

★ To reach these lakes from downtown Denver, take I-25 south and exit on Hampden Avenue (U.S. 285). Head west on 285, which eventually becomes a divided highway. Turn left (south) on Wadsworth Boulevard and drive approximately one mile to West Quincy Avenue. Turn right (west) on West Quincy and drive one-half mile to the lakes.

THE LOWER FOOTHILLS

Red Rocks Park

Red Rocks Park, part of Denver's Mountain Park system, is located in the lower foothills, west of Metro Denver. This park, centered around a collection of huge sandstone formations, is an excellent place to study the fauna and flora of the Pinyon-Juniper Zone. The picturesque setting is unfortunately a favorite hangout for the "beer and wine crowd," and their cans and bottles decorate the shrubbery. Nevertheless, the park remains an interesting spot for birders.

Certain birds, such as scrub jays, crows, northern flickers, magpies and black-capped chickadees are common here throughout the year. Rock doves have adapted to this area, roosting and nesting in the many "pigeonholes" that dot the sandstone monoliths.

With the arrival of spring Bullock's orioles, lazuli buntings, Virginia's warblers and black-headed grosbeaks return to claim their nesting sites. Standing above any one of the ravines on a morning in June, the birder is subjected to sensory overload. Orioles, yellow-breasted chats, scrub jays, cowbirds and towhees provide a background chorus of chirps, trills and whistles. Flashes of color from yellow warblers, Bullock's orioles, lazuli buntings, chats and other songbirds brighten the thickets. Squadrons of cliff swallows and white-throated swifts swoop and dive above one's head.

Vesper and lark sparrows are fairly common on the open grassland during the warmer months. Lesser goldfinches and Say's phoebes are occasionally common along the roadways. Barn swallows are abundant along the streams that traverse the lower grassland. Hawks, especially red-tails, often soar above the ridges, joined by golden eagles during the colder months. If you remain until dusk, you will be treated to the mellow call of the poorwills as they get ready for a night of hunting.

Plan to return to Red Rocks in early October. The fall colors are generally at their peak; scrub oaks have turned a brilliant orange and autumn yellows contrast with the dark junipers, which nestle against the red sandstone cliffs. All of this color shines in the bright October sun and is set against the backdrop of a clear, blue sky. Cool autumn winds bring dark-eyed juncos, Cassin's finches and occasional flocks of red crossbills to the Red Rocks area. Townsend's solitaires, descending from the higher mountains, winter here in large numbers.

As heavy snows blanket the Front Range,

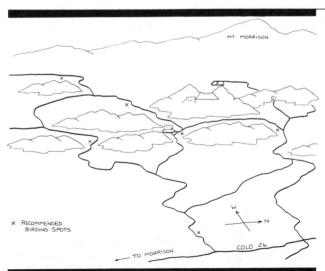

RED ROCKS PARK

MT. MORRISON

x RECOMMENDED
BIRDING SPOTS

TO MORRISON

COLO 26

Red Rocks Park.

other birds arrive to forage and roost along the lower slopes. These include mountain chickadees, brown creepers and, less reliably, rosy finches. Large numbers of robins winter in the park, feeding on the plentiful berries. They are occasionally joined by flocks of waxwings (Bohemian and cedar), which travel along the foothills during the colder months. Back in the sandstone caverns canyon wrens, remaining through the winter, noisily hunt for insects.

I have found that Red Rocks Park is one of the better places to find northern shrikes during the winter months. These birds are typically found perched atop a small tree or juniper bush, scanning the surrounding grassland for field mice. Look for them on the open scrub-grassland, just east of the rock formations.

In addition to the birds discussed above, Red Rocks provides food and shelter for a variety of mammals. Most conspicuous are the rock squirrels and chipmunks that scamper over the sandstone.

Mule deer, common along the foothills, are often
seen during the late winter and early spring. Look for
them on the flanks of Mt. Morrison, just west of the
park, or on the hogback ridge, east of Red Rocks.

To reach Red Rocks Park from Denver, take ★
I-70 west. Upon entering the foothills, take the Red
Rocks/Morrison exit. Head south toward Morrison
on Colorado Route 26 (Hogback Road). Entrance
roads lead into the Park, as shown on the map.
There is no fee.

South Mesa/Shadow Canyon Trails

The Mesa Trail winds through the lower foothills
from Eldorado Springs to the western edge of
Boulder. The area discussed below is limited to the
southernmost one and one-half miles of this trail
and the loop that it forms with the Shadow
Canyon Trail.

From the parking area off Colorado Route 170,
the Mesa Trail first crosses South Boulder Creek
and then winds northward across a scrub-grassland,
broken by thickets and rock formations. During the
summer months rufous-sided and green-tailed
towhees are abundant here, scratching for seeds
and insects among the scrub oaks. Rock wrens are
also common, feeding along the boulders that dot
the grassland. Western meadowlarks, magpies,
mourning doves and the grassland sparrows
(vesper, lark and savannah) are found on the
prairie during the warmer months. By late September white-crowned sparrows, Lincoln's sparrows
and Wilson's warblers, having descended from the
mountains, gather in the oak thickets.

Due to the rocky, varied topography, this is an
excellent area for observing the many hawks and
falcons that inhabit our region. Red-tailed hawks,
ferruginous hawks and occasional golden eagles
may be found at any time of the year. Swainson's
hawks are often seen during the summer, replaced
by rough-legged hawks during the colder months.

Kestrels are common here, often hunting from the power lines that cross the area. Prairie falcons may be seen as they swoop along the grasslands, while Cooper's and sharp-shinned hawks are often found gliding along the wooded mesas.

South Mesa Trail.

After slowly climbing northward for about one-half mile, the trail angles toward the west, entering an area of scattered ponderosa pines. Northern flickers, magpies and Steller's jays are common here throughout the year. Looking off to the northwest, you will likely see mule deer browsing on the foothill grasslands or resting under the pines. They are especially common during the colder months, when snows force them down from higher terrain.

As the trail climbs higher, the pine forest thickens. Mountain chickadees, pygmy nuthatches, downy woodpeckers and brown creepers are found here, especially in fall and winter. Look for red-breasted nuthatches in late summer, as they move down from the higher forests. By early November, flocks of red crossbills, Cassin's finches and dark-eyed juncos are common in this region. In fact, this is an excellent area to find white-winged juncos during the late fall and winter months. Saw-whet and pygmy owls may also be found here during the colder months; look for them roosting in clusters of small pine trees.

At the top of the ridge, the Mesa Trail angles northward while a short trail continues westward and downhill, forming a link with the Shadow Canyon Trail. Before descending through the canyon, follow the trail farther up and westward for a hundred yards or so. Here, in the upper reaches of Shadow Canyon, huge rock formations jut from the canyon walls. Canyon wrens are found here throughout the year. During summer look for yellow-bellied marmots as they sun themselves on the boulders. Townsend's solitaires can be found in this wooded canyon in all seasons, but are most common from September through April. In the winter, flocks of bushtits and rosy finches occasionally roam through the area, though their presence is quite erratic. Turkey vultures soar along the cliffs during the warmer months, replaced by ravens during the winter.

While the Mesa Trail represents the high and dry route, the return trip through Shadow Canyon takes the birder through moist thickets and lush shrubbery. Indeed, the trail is almost overgrown during the summer months. The moist habitat attracts many of the warblers, flycatchers and other songbirds that summer in the lower foothills. Look for Virginia's and MacGillivray's warblers, black-headed grosbeaks, lazuli buntings and yellow-breasted chats. Western wood pewees and western flycatchers hunt from the trees that border the ravine. During the colder months dark-eyed juncos (all four subspecies), mountain chickadees and pygmy nuthatches are often abundant here. Flocks of cedar and Bohemian waxwings occasionally stop by to feed on the numerous berries that grow in the canyon, most often in late winter or early spring.

**SOUTH MESA TRAIL
AND SHADOW
CANYON**

*1. Mesa Trail
2. Rock Formations
3. Shadow Canyon*

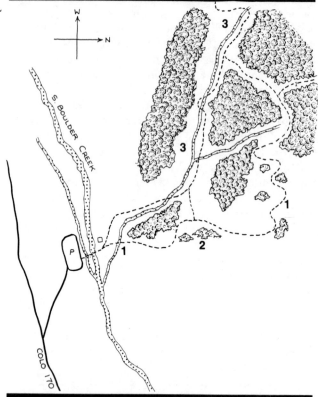

★   To reach this area from Denver, take I-25
north and exit onto U.S. 36 which heads northwest,
toward Boulder. After driving 13.5 miles on U.S.
36, take the Superior-Louisville Exit. Turn left,
crossing the highway and then take an immediate
right, following Colorado 170 westward toward
Marshall and Eldorado Springs. After driving 3.9
miles, cross over Colorado 93 and drive another
1.6 miles on Colorado 170. A gravel drive leads
down to the parking area on the right (north) side
of the road.

    From Boulder, take Broadway south. This
street eventually becomes an open highway (Colorado 93). Take it south and exit right (west) onto
Colorado 170, toward Eldorado Canyon State
Park. Drive 1.6 miles to the parking area.

Gregory Canyon

Gregory Canyon is a beautiful rocky ravine in the Front Range foothills, just west of Boulder. Since it is a relatively young canyon, the gorge is narrow and the grade is fairly steep. Elevation gain from the parking area to the top of the ridge is approximately 800 feet.

A visit to Gregory Canyon on a summer morning offers both a pleasant hike and excellent birding. The trail initially winds through an area of lush shrubbery and moist thickets. Insects are numerous here, attracting the resident flycatchers and warblers. These include Virginia's and MacGillivray's warblers, ovenbirds, dusky and western flycatchers and western wood pewees. Joining these hunters are the broad-tailed hummingbirds, which move among the flowering shrubs in search of nectar. After walking for a hundred yards or so, bear right and upward, as the trail climbs across the dry, sunny slope of the canyon's northern wall. Rufous-sided and green-tailed towhees are common in the thickets, the latter often emerging to run ahead of you on the trail. Rock and canyon wrens forage along the boulders that jut from the canyon walls.

Approximately one-third of the way up the canyon, the trail angles to the left and dips to cross the stream. This is an excellent spot to stop and watch the various warblers, flycatchers and vireos that summer in the canyon. Beyond this stream-crossing the trail climbs rather steeply. Here the ponderosa pine forest thickens and the seed-eaters predominate. Mountain chickadees, nuthatches (all three species), Steller's jays, and brown creepers are present throughout the year. They are joined by chipping sparrows, lesser goldfinches and black-headed grosbeaks during the warmer months. Northern flickers and downy and hairy woodpeckers noisily move about the forest as turkey vultures glide silently overhead. Scan the distant cliffs for Cooper's and sharp-shinned hawks, which soar along the treetops hunting for careless songbirds.

THE FOOTHILL CANYONS

*View from a switch-
back, Upper Gregory
Canyon.*

Returning to the canyon in winter, the visitor
is greeted by noisy flocks of black-capped chickadees. Joining them in the lower canyon are dark-
eyed juncos arrived from the north, and mountain
chickadees, nuthatches and creepers that have
descended from the higher mountain forests. Townsend's solitaires are common in the canyon during
the colder months. Replacing the vultures that have
gone south, ravens scavenge along the canyon
walls. If you're lucky you may spot a saw-whet or
pygmy owl roosting in the small pines that line the
trail. Rare spotted owls have also been found here.
Depending upon the cone crop, Cassin's finches,
red crossbills, pine grosbeaks and evening grosbeaks may be found in the upper canyon.

As in most ecosystems May is a time of transition in Gregory Canyon. Late spring snows overlap
with the thunderstorms of summer, providing
plenty of moisture for the wildflowers to bloom
and the insects to breed. By mid-May, Virginia's
and MacGillivray's warblers, solitary vireos and
western wood pewees are returning to feast on the
emerging insects. Flocks of pine siskins move
through the upper canyon, on their way to breed in
the mountain forests. Lesser goldfinches, broad-

tailed hummingbirds and the mountain flycatchers generally arrive in late May.

Gregory Canyon is also home to the many small mammals that characterize the Front Range foothills. Rock squirrels and chipmunks are especially common; since they do not hibernate, they are often seen on sunny winter days. Yellow-bellied marmots may be encountered during the warmer months but sleep away the winter in their underground dens. Red squirrels, active throughout the year, are fairly common in the upper canyon forest.

To reach Gregory Canyon from Denver, take

GREGORY CANYON

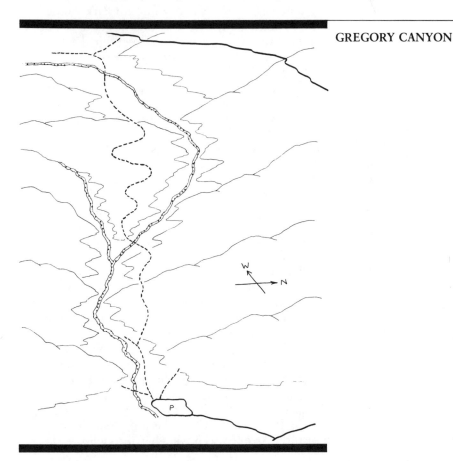

I-25 north and then U.S. 36 toward Boulder. After reaching Boulder, exit west on Baseline Road. At the very base of the foothills, turn left onto a dirt-gravel road that leads to the Gregory Canyon parking area.

Waterton Canyon

The headwaters of the South Platte River lie in the high alpine meadows of the Mosquito Range in central Colorado. After tumbling through mountain forests, the river's tributaries meander southeastward across the grasslands of South Park to the Pike's Peak region, where the South Platte has been dammed to form Eleven-Mile Reservoir. Exiting the reservoir, the river angles northeast and slices through the foothills.

Waterton Canyon represents the South Platte's final journey through the Rockies before it rumbles onto the plains of eastern Colorado. The canyon was recently reopened to the public following completion of the Strontia Springs Dam, which sits six miles up from the canyon's mouth. A dirt-gravel roadbed parallels the river as it winds through the canyon. The road is closed to motorized vehicles (except for official use) but is open to the public for hiking, biking and horseback riding. Dogs are not permitted in the canyon due to the resident bighorn sheep and deer populations.

Due to its age and the size of the stream that formed it, Waterton Canyon is a relatively wide gorge and the grade is gentle. A hike up the canyon offers an excellent study in the effects that elevation and sun exposure have on vegetation and, thus, on local wildlife populations. The visitor will notice that the north-facing slopes are well forested while the south-facing walls are characterized by dry, rocky soil, with scattered shrubs and thickets. On these sunny slopes trees grow primarily along the shaded ravines, where the soil retains more moisture. As one ascends higher through the canyon, the Pinyon-Juniper Zone gives way to forests of ponderosa pine and Douglas–fir. By visiting during the different seasons, the birder will also witness the phenomenon of vertical migration, as certain birds move up and down the canyon with changes in climate (and secondary variations in food supply).

Waterton Canyon's bird population is perhaps most diverse in early summer. From the parking area the trail initially traverses a flat area, characterized by dense thickets, shallow ponds and groves of cottonwood trees. In summer Bullock's orioles, American goldfinches, house wrens and lazuli buntings are common here. Magpies, black-capped chickadees and northern flickers are present throughout the year. Belted kingfishers noisily hunt along the South Platte and numerous swallows (barn, tree and cliff) swoop above the river, feasting on insects.

Autumn snow, Waterton Canyon.

In the lower canyon scrub jays and lesser goldfinches are usually common along the wooded
ravines. Rufous-sided towhees, catbirds and yellow
warblers feed among the thickets. Rock wrens,
common but widely scattered, bob along the
boulder fields. Present yearlong, canyon wrens are
usually found on the larger rock formations that jut
from the canyon's walls. Kestrels, merlins and
prairie falcons, which nest on the steep cliffs, hunt
for birds and mice along the lower slopes.

Higher in the canyon, where the forest thickens,
Steller's jays, mountain chickadees, nuthatches and
pine siskins are usually found. Violet-green
swallows, often joined by white-throated swifts,
move about in large flocks. During the warmer
months turkey vultures glide high overhead, riding
the thermals and searching the ground for carrion.
Golden eagles, present throughout the year, are
often seen in the late morning hours as they soar
above the canyon.

By September the first signs of autumn are
evident. Cool winds blow down the canyon and light
snows may blanket the foothills. Large flocks of
Townsend's solitaires begin to arrive, descending
from the higher forests. Lesser goldfinches and rock
wrens seem more abundant as they gather in flocks
prior to their fall migration.

Returning in November the visitor confronts
the cold, windy environment of winter in the foothill canyons. Nevertheless, many birds are still to
be found. Magpies, crows, scrub jays and starlings
scavenge along the lower flats. Black-capped chickadees, tree sparrows, juncos and song sparrows feed
in the thickets that line the river. Check the cottonwoods for northern flickers, downy woodpeckers
and great horned owls. Lewis' woodpeckers, though
erratic, may also be found. Red-tailed hawks and
kestrels, perched in the cottonwoods, scan the
clearings for mice.

In the canyon the birder will find Townsend's
solitaires, scrub and Steller's jays, canyon wrens
and mountain chickadees. Flocks of rosy finches

and bushtits may take refuge here during the colder months. Dippers, which can be found in the canyon yearlong, are especially common from November through April. Look for them just below the Marston Diversion, approximately three miles up the canyon. Here they are often found walking along the concrete structures, intermittently plunging into the cold, turbulent river.

In addition to the birds, the visitor will find a diversity of mammals in Waterton Canyon. Most popular are the bighorn sheep, which, due to an outbreak of pneumonia, have declined numerically in recent years. Look for them on south-facing

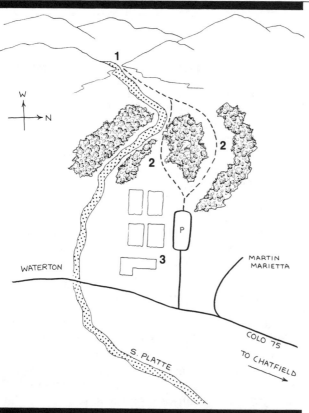

WATERTON CANYON
1. *The Canyon*
2. *Lower Flats*
3. *Water Treatment Plant*

slopes in the lower canyon. If you visit in November, you will likely see mixed herds of males and females and, since this is their rutting season, you may witness the famous head-jolting duels of the males. Mule deer are also common here, favoring the greener north-facing slopes. They are best seen during the evening hours. Many small mammals live in the canyon, including chipmunks, rock squirrels and skunks.

★   To reach Waterton Canyon take Colorado Route 75 southwest from Chatfield Reservoir (see map). Bear left as you reach the hogback (rather than bearing right into Martin Marietta). After turning left drive approximately 15 yards and turn right into the Waterton Canyon parking area. If possible, plan to visit on a weekday since this popular area can be crowded on weekends.

THE UPPER FOOTHILLS

Green Mountain Trail

With an elevation of 8144 feet, Green Mountain is one of the highest points in Boulder Mountain Parks. From this summit one has a spectacular view of the Front Range (from Mt. Evans to the Mummy Range), the surrounding foothills and the eastern plains. The West Ridge Trail is the easiest route to the top and also provides excellent birding along the way.

The West Ridge Trail begins at an elevation of approximately 7600 feet and roller-coasters its way along a gentle slope for most of its length, before climbing steeply to the summit. In doing so the trail dips in and out of a dense, transitional forest, crossing open meadows with scattered trees and rock formations. Mixed with the living Douglas–fir and ponderosa pine, there are plenty of dead trees and fallen timber, very attractive to the woodpeckers that characterize this zone. Indeed, it is one of the best areas in our region to look for hairy woodpeckers and Williamson's sapsuckers.

Arriving on a crisp October morning, the birder

will find flocks of pygmy nuthatches noisily roaming from tree to tree, rivaled in number only by the mountain chickadees. White-breasted and red-breasted nuthatches are also common, adding their distinctive voices to the morning chorus. Less conspicuous and far less gregarious are the brown creepers, patiently hunting for insects as they circle up treetrunks. Downy and hairy woodpeckers hammer away at rotting logs, as dark-eyed juncos forage for seeds among the fallen branches. Townsend's solitaires sing from the treetops, while Steller's jays and crows noisily cruise the area. On the open meadows western and mountain bluebirds, soon to depart for their wintering grounds, hunt for insects and berries. Blue grouse may be encountered on the grassy slopes.

As the days shorten and the snows arrive, many of the birds head south or move down to the plains. However, most of them are well equipped to remain through the winter. Returning in January the visitor will find that the nuthatches, chickadees and creepers are still here, seemingly oblivious to the cold. Northern flickers and hairy woodpeckers feast on wood beetles that hibernate in the dead trees. Flocks of red crossbills and evening grosbeaks, roaming along the foothill forests, are often seen. Pine grosbeaks, which flock during the winter, are also fairly common. Goshawks, descending from the higher mountains, may be encountered as they hunt along the ridge. On the meadows look for northern shrikes as they perch on small trees, scanning the ground for rodents. This is also a good time of year to see the resident mule deer, which find ample browse along this sunny, windswept ridge.

By early April the western and mountain bluebirds are returning and have started to nest. As the days pass the air becomes alive with the drumming and raucous calls of the resident woodpeckers, doing their best to attract mates and establish territories. These macho displays peak in mid-April when northern flickers, hairy woodpeckers and

Open transition forest cloaks the West Ridge of Green Mountain.

Williamson's sapsuckers all vie for attention. White-breasted nuthatches are also quite noisy and aggressive at this time. Ignoring all of this, flocks of mountain chickadees and pygmy nuthatches roam about the area. Townsend's solitaires flycatch along the forest borders, and turkey vultures, returning from their winter in the south, soar gracefully overhead. Cooper's and sharp-shinned hawks may be seen as they swoop above the trees, hunting for songbirds. Gray-headed juncos, having moved up from the nearby canyons, canvas the ground for seeds and begin to nest in the forest margins.

By June this open woodland has settled into its summer patterns. Cavity nesters, including violet-green swallows, western and mountain bluebirds and the various woodpeckers, tend to their newly-hatched young. Olive-sided flycatchers are found here, repeating their distinctive three-note call from the tops of dead trees. In the trees that border the meadows Townsend's solitaires, western wood pewees, chipping sparrows and yellow-rumped warblers hunt for insects. Broad-tailed humming-birds, though more common in the nearby canyons,

may also be found as they move among the wildflowers. Pine siskins roam about in large flocks,
outnumbering the mountain chickadees which have
dispersed into the higher mountain forests. Steller's
jays and pygmy nuthatches, favoring Transition
Zone woodlands, are still present in good numbers.

To reach Green Mountain Trail from Denver,
take I-25 north and exit onto U.S. 36 toward
Boulder. After entering Boulder turn left (west) on
Baseline Road and drive until it ends at the base of
the foothills. Bear right onto the paved road that
leads up through the Boulder Mountain Parks.
Follow this road for 4.7 miles as it winds up and
gradually southwestward. Just before the road exits

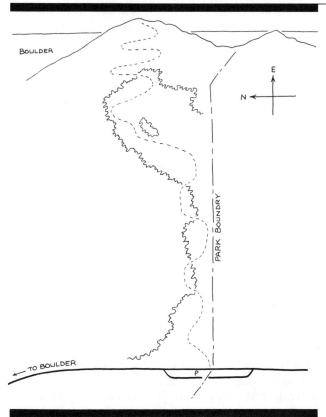

GREEN MOUNTAIN
TRAIL

the Parks (marked by sign: "Leaving Boulder Mountain Parks") look for a graveled parking lane on the right (west) side of the road. The trailhead is just across the road from this parking area (see map). The trail described above is officially recognized as the Green Mountain–West Ridge Trail.

Mt. Falcon Park

Mt. Falcon Park is part of the Jefferson County Open Space system. This park is essentially a 7600-foot-high meadow, bordered by coniferous forest and rugged, rocky cliffs. It sits on a broad plateau in the Front Range foothills, flanked by Bear Creek and Turkey Creek Canyons, southwest of Denver.

From the parking area the visitor has an expansive view of the surrounding foothills and a spectacular view of Denver and the eastern Colorado plains. The park has an excellent network of hiking and horseback trails, some of which are illustrated on the map. This area is also popular for cross-country skiing in winter. The varied terrain is home to a wide variety of birds and other wildlife, including mule deer, bobcat, Abert's squirrels and other small mammals. In addition to the natural beauty, the park is of interest from an historical point of view, with ruins of a mansion and the site for a planned "Western White House" located on the northeast rim of the plateau.

Though all areas of Mt. Falcon Park are excellent for birding, the following discussion will be limited to the Parmalee Trail, including the return hike across the central meadow. This route takes the birder through all of the major habitats found within the park. The Parmalee Trail originates approximately fifty yards from the parking area, heading off to the south (see map). After skirting a small meadow, the trail plunges into a forest of ponderosa pine and Douglas–fir. As the trail winds down through this forest, it intermittently crosses brushy clearings and thicket-lined ravines. This section of the park usually abounds with Steller's jays, mountain chickadees, rufous-sided towhees and gray-headed juncos. Hairy woodpeckers, pygmy and white-breasted nuthatches, pine siskins and Townsend's solitaires are also common here. Since they favor open woodlands, this is a good place to find Cooper's hawks, especially in late summer. During the warmer months look for yellow warblers, Virginia's and MacGillivray's warblers, house wrens and western wood pewees feeding along the ravines. In the early evening hours, especially on cool autumn days, scan the nearby slopes for wild turkeys as they forage in the clearings. During the winter dark-eyed juncos gather in the sheltered ravines and flocks of red crossbills, evening grosbeaks and Cassin's finches stop by to feast on the pine seeds.

Emerging from the canopy of trees, the trail turns eastward, crossing the dry, rocky slope that

The Parmalee Trail.

MT. FALCON PARK

1. *Parmalee Trail*
2. *Central Meadow*
3. *Mansion Ruins*

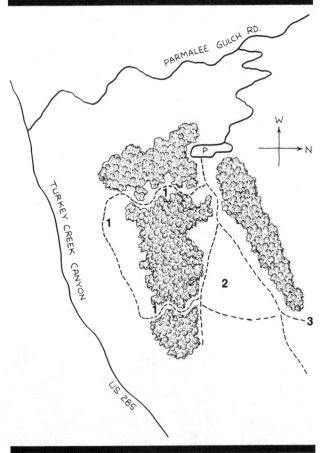

forms the southern border of the park and the
northern wall of Turkey Creek Canyon. This sun-
scorched area is studded with small shrubs, scrub
oak and rock formations. During the warmer
months rufous-sided and green-tailed towhees,
black-headed grosbeaks and rock wrens forage
along the slope. Steller's and scrub jays are present
throughout the year. In late summer look for black-
throated gray warblers, orange-crowned warblers
and band-tailed pigeons. The latter are often
encountered in large flocks, feeding among the

thickets or roosting in the scattered trees. Blue grouse favor such sunny slopes and, especially in early fall, may flush from the hillside as you pass by.

This section of the trail offers a spectacular view of Turkey Creek Canyon and is a good area to look for the birds of prey that hunt along the foothills. These include prairie falcons, merlins, kestrels, red-tailed hawks, Cooper's hawks, sharp-shinned hawks and occasional golden eagles. Turkey vultures soar along the cliffs during the warmer months and, in winter, goshawks may be seen here.

After traversing the canyon wall the Parmalee Trail climbs back through the open forest, emerging at the southern edge of the park's central meadow. Magpies are common here throughout the year, joined by mourning doves in summer. Western and mountain bluebirds are found from April to early October, hunting from the low shrubs that dot the meadow. Their numbers increase dramatically in late summer, as they gather in flocks prior to the autumn migration. In the warmer months chipping sparrows, lesser goldfinches, western tanagers and yellow-rumped warblers feed in the trees that border the meadow, wary of the sharp-shinned hawks that often glide overhead.

As mentioned above, Abert's squirrels are found in Mt. Falcon's forests. These long-eared squirrels occur in two color phases (black and gray). Favoring the Transition Zone, Abert's squirrels tend to localize in limited areas of our foothills and Mt. Falcon is one of the better spots to find them. The resident mule deer are most often found on the open meadows or along Turkey Creek Canyon, especially during evening. Though bobcats live here, attested to by their prints and droppings along the trails, they are very secretive, mostly nocturnal and rarely seen. Rock squirrels and golden-mantled ground squirrels are fairly common along the Parmalee Trail, especially on rocky slopes.

To reach Mt. Falcon Park, take U.S. 285 ★ southwest from Denver. After entering the foothills,

drive 2.5 miles past the Evergreen-Red Rocks Park
Exit. Turn right onto Parmalee Gulch Road. After
winding northward for 2.7 miles, turn right onto a
dirt-gravel road that winds up through a small
residential area. Follow the "Mt. Falcon Park" signs
and drive 1.7 miles to the parking area at the top
of the ridge. There is no entrance fee.

MOUNTAIN FORESTS & TUNDRA

Guanella Pass

Guanella Pass is a scenic alpine ridge that connects
the Mt. Evans group with the Continental Divide.
It is located approximately thirteen road miles
south of Georgetown, Colorado. Elevation at the
pass is 11,669 feet.

While this area is not in the immediate Denver-
Boulder region, it is easily accessible throughout
the year and offers some unique birding opportunities. To local birders and naturalists, Guanella Pass
is best known for the large number of white-tailed
ptarmigan that gather there during the winter and
early spring. This flock, thought to be one of the
largest and most concentrated to be found in the
lower forty-eight states, is attracted here by the
plentiful willow shrubs.

★ To reach Guanella Pass, take I-70 west from
Denver. After entering the foothills, drive 31 miles
to the Georgetown Exit (228). Turn left, crossing
under I-70 and then right into town. The pass road
winds up from the southwestern end of town.

The lower section of this road, from Georgetown to the hydroelectric plant, is paved. Unfortunately, the beauty of this lower area is marred by
power lines and other man-made structures. But
above the power plant, as you enter the Arapahoe
National Forest, the pavement and the power lines
disappear. Here, especially along the right (west)
side of the road, an extensive aspen forest begins,
providing a brilliant display in early October.
During the warm months check these deciduous
woodlands for yellow-bellied sapsuckers, hermit

thrushes, white-breasted nuthatches and olive-sided flycatchers.

As the road climbs higher the conifers again predominate. Numerous beaver ponds are found along the road. These shallow pools, surrounded by willows and shaded by groves of Engelmann spruce, attract the many birds that inhabit this zone. In summer Lincoln's sparrows, white-crowned sparrows and Wilson's warblers nest among the willows. Mountain chickadees and Steller's jays, present throughout the year, are joined by large flocks of pine siskins and yellow-rumped warblers in summer. Gray-headed juncos, ruby-crowned and golden-crowned kinglets and Townsend's solitaires are also common here. Entering the upper reaches of the mountain forest, the road crosses through grassy meadows with scattered trees. This high, open forest attracts pine grosbeaks, Hammond's flycatchers, gray jays and Clarke's nutcrackers.

As you approach timberline, watch for Cassin's finches feeding along the road. These large finches,

Summer storm above Guanella Pass.

favoring stunted, alpine woodlands during summer, move down to the foothills and plains in winter.

Near the pass the road crosses onto the open, rocky tundra. Dense mats of willow thickets dot the landscape, providing food, shelter and nesting sites for the birds that inhabit this beautiful yet harsh environment. White-crowned sparrows and water pipits are abundant here during the summer. Ravens scavenge along this ridge throughout the year and, as discussed above, white-tailed ptarmigan gather here during the colder months. High, rugged peaks rise to the east and west of the pass, including Mt. Bierstadt, one of Colorado's "fourteeners," just to the southeast.

The southern side of Guanella Pass is drained by Duck Creek, which tumbles down into the Geneva Basin. Rather than backtrack to Georgetown, I suggest that you head south through this beautiful, forested canyon. There are many picnic areas and trailheads along the road. Watch for dippers along the streams, common here from late spring through October.

This scenic route eventually brings you to Grant, Colorado. Turn left on U.S. 285 and head northeast back to Denver.

Mt. Evans Area

Mt. Evans, at 14,264 feet, is the 13th highest peak in Colorado. The drive to this lofty summit offers not only spectacular mountain scenery but an exciting and convenient way to view the flora and fauna of a striking, rarefied world. The route from Bergen Park to Summit Lake takes the visitor through the various zones of the mountain forests and onto the windswept, treeless tundra. All areas are easily viewed from pull-offs or parking areas along the road and extensive walking, not recommended for the unconditioned visitor, is unnecessary.

Colorado Route 103, from Bergen Park to Echo Lake and back down to Idaho Springs, is open throughout the year. Colorado Route 5, from Echo Lake to Summit Lake, is usually open from late May through September, depending on snow conditions. The stretch of Colorado 5 from Summit Lake to the summit of Mt. Evans is generally open from mid-June until Labor Day.

A few points should be made for those un-accustomed to travel in the high mountains. All other factors being equal, the mean air temperature drops three degrees Fahrenheit for every 1000 feet gain in elevation. In addition wind is a constant companion of these high peaks, adding to the chilling effects of the air and the burning power of the sun. With regard to the latter, the thin air permits more ultra-violet light to reach the skin and if prolonged outdoor activity is planned a sunscreen is advised. Furthermore, the rarefied air is low in oxygen content and, for those unconditioned to these altitudes, extensive walking should be avoided. In a nutshell, conditions on Mt. Evans cannot be predicted from Denver. But if prepared with extra

Chief Mountain looms above Squaw Pass Road.

clothing, sunscreen and common sense you will very much enjoy your visit.

★ Snowmelt is in full force and spring migrants are returning to the high country by late May. This is a good time to visit the Mt. Evans region. Take I-70 west from Denver. After entering the foothills, drive 7 miles to the El Rancho exit (Exit 252). Turn left, taking Colorado 74 toward Bergen Park and Evergreen. Drive 2.5 miles and bear right onto Colorado 103, which leads toward Echo Lake and Mt. Evans.

MT. EVANS AREA
1. *Mt. Evans*
2. *Summit Lake*
3. *Mt. Goliath*
   Bristlecone Pine Area
4. *Echo Lake*
5. *Chief Mountain*
6. *Squaw Mountain*
7. *Meadow at 9200 ft.*

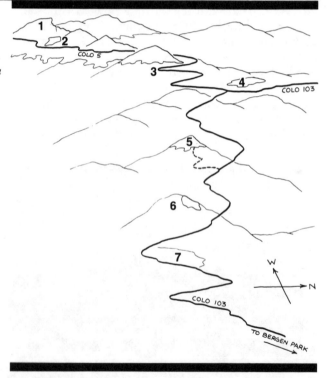

After driving through the picnic grounds you will pass a large open grassland on your left. This is the northern end of Mean's Meadow, which is a major calving grounds for elk in our region. Scan the forest margin along the far edge of the meadow, where elk often graze during the winter and spring.

Births usually occur in May or June. In addition
to the elk, western and mountain bluebirds are
frequently seen on the grassland.

After driving for 7 miles up Colorado 103 you
will reach a small, fenced meadow lined with
aspen, small conifers and gnarled willow thickets.
Elevation here is 9200 feet. Look for ruby-crowned
kinglets, Wilson's and yellow-rumped warblers,
gray-headed juncos, chipping sparrows and pine
siskins feeding in the thickets. Yellow-bellied
sapsuckers are also found here, favoring the
deciduous trees.

Colorado 103 continues to wind upward and
westward through dense conifer forest. At Squaw
Pass the road levels out and snakes along the
northern flanks of Squaw and Chief Mountains,
offering a spectacular view of the Front Range.
Along the road there are many pull-offs and picnic
areas where you may wish to stop to rest, eat,
enjoy the scenery or do some leisurely birding. If
you do break out the food, count on gray jays and
golden-mantled ground squirrels to turn up for
handouts. The birds of the high mountain forests
are often seen around these picnic areas or along
the short trails that lead into the woods. Included
are mountain chickadees, ruby-crowned and golden-
crowned kinglets, gray jays, Clarke's nutcrackers,
white-breasted and red-breasted nuthatches, hermit
thrushes, Townsend's solitaires and evening grosbeaks. Ravens scavenge along Squaw Pass Road
throughout the year.

For the more adventurous (and conditioned)
birder, a trail leads to the summit of Chief Mountain, offering spectacular scenery and good birding
along the way. Look for the trail marker two miles
beyond the 10,000 feet sign, along the road. The
trail winds through the upper reaches of the Canadian and Hudsonian forests. In addition to the
birds mentioned above, look for three-toed woodpeckers, veeries and pine grosbeaks. If you're lucky
you may spot a pygmy owl roosting in the conifers.
The trail eventually leads onto the rocky tundra,
where pikas scamper over the boulders and gray-

headed juncos forage for seeds in the crevices. Check along the stunted timberline forest for Cassin's finches, Hammond's flycatchers and yellow-rumped warblers. Blue grouse and white-tailed ptarmigan are occasionally seen as they forage among the thickets.

Proceed westward on Colorado 103 to Echo Lake, which sits on this high ridge at an elevation of 10,600 feet. Ambling through the picnic grounds, at the north end of the lake, you will likely encounter gray jays, ravens, yellow-rumped warblers and mountain chickadees. Red squirrels put up a fuss if you get too close to their favorite tree. Along the lake white-crowned sparrows, Wilson's warblers and Lincoln's sparrows nest in the willow thickets.

Colorado 5, beginning at Echo Lake, leads up through the highest reaches of the Hudsonian forest and onto the open tundra. Near timberline a small, uneven parking area will be noted on the left side of the road. This serves the Mt. Goliath Bristlecone Pine Area, and is a good place to stop and enjoy the birds and other wildlife that inhabit this stunted forest. The ancient bristlecone pines provide food, shelter and perching branches for a wide variety of birds. These include gray-headed juncos, Ham-

Echo Lake.

Summer snow at Summit Lake.

mond's and olive-sided flycatchers, mountain blue-birds, yellow-rumped and Wilson's warblers, Clarke's nutcrackers, white-crowned sparrows, and Cassin's finches.

Summit Lake sits in a beautiful cirque on the northeastern face of Mt. Evans. Elevation here is 12,830 feet. While this is an excellent spot to stop and explore the tundra, bitter winds are common here and warm dress is advised. Water pipits are usually abundant, bobbing along the rocky shore. Brown-capped rosy finches nest on the cliffs surrounding the lake but are often hard to find. At other times they appear in large flocks, searching for seeds and insects along the snowbanks. Common ravens often soar along the adjacent cliffs and prairie falcons and northern goshawks are occasionally seen hunting for rodents and grouse. Pikas are common here, their high-pitched cries echoing across the cirque. Look for them on the slope just south of the lake. Mountain goats also seem to favor this area and are often found north of Summit Lake, where the terrain plummets into the Chicago Basin.

Plan to return to the Mt. Evans area in early July. Not only will you have a second chance to find the birds that you missed in the spring, but the alpine wildflowers will be at their peak. Summer is also a good time to find the larger mammals that inhabit this region. If possible, visit in the late afternoon and evening hours when these mountain residents are most active. Mountain goats and big-horn sheep roam in the steeper areas. They often turn up along the road, oblivious to your presence. Mule deer and elk, moving to higher terrain during the warmer months, are often seen in open forest, especially in the zone just below timberline. Yellow-bellied marmots, most active in the late afternoon, are frequently found along the Mt. Evans Road.

Winter returns to the high country by late September. Actually, snow may fall on the higher peaks at any time of the year. But a visit to this region on a sunny winter day can be very pleasant indeed, including a wide variety of birds. Mountain chickadees, white-breasted nuthatches, golden-crowned kinglets, gray jays and Clarke's nutcrackers still roam the mountain forests. Hairy and three-toed woodpeckers, undaunted by the snow and cold, chisel away at the dead trees, searching for beetles. Pygmy owls and northern goshawks still patrol the meadows, feeding on the red squirrels and snowshoe hares that remain active through winter. Rosy finches (all three species) are occasionally found along Squaw Pass Road, especially from late October through November. Ravens, raucous as ever, scavenge for roadkills and feed on the carcasses of deer and elk that succumb to the winter snows.

Backyard Birding

Backyard birding, though not as exhilarating as a hike through the forest, can be both interesting and productive, especially if your yard has a good variety of foliage and you take an active role in attracting birds with feeders, bird baths, etc. The novice birder is usually not aware of the large num-ber and variety of birds frequenting residential habitats. In our region, there are at least thirty species that are fairly common in the typical back-yard during at least part of the year.

Many birds inhabit our residential areas throughout the year. These include house sparrows, blue jays, northern flickers, house finches, robins, crows, starlings and black-capped chickadees. In summer these birds are joined by mourning doves, grackles, American goldfinches and house wrens.

Spring migration is a good time to watch for the many songbirds that move through our urban areas on their way to breeding grounds in the mountains and grasslands. In late April and early May look for pine siskins, yellow-rumped warblers, chipping sparrows and white-crowned sparrows. By mid-May Bullock's orioles, yellow warblers, lazuli buntings, western tanagers, broad-tailed humming-birds and various flycatchers stop by.

Other birds, while not alighting in your yard, may be seen as they pass overhead. Great blue and black-crowned night herons are often spotted on summer evenings as they move from their rookeries to feeding grounds. In late summer, especially from late August through September, look for flocks of Franklin's gulls and nighthawks as they roam above the city, feasting on insects. Canada geese and ring-billed gulls, though present throughout the year, are most common during the colder months.

In winter and early spring cold and snow force many birds down from the mountains or in from the prairies, and, if you provide seeds and suet for them, a good variety will turn up. Among the more common visitors are black-capped and mountain chickadees, house finches, dark-eyed juncos, downy woodpeckers, red-breasted nuthatches and brown creepers. Less common but occasionally abundant are red crossbills, evening grosbeaks and Cassin's finches. If berry-producing shrubs are present, look for flocks of Bohemian and cedar waxwings.

The variety of birds at backyard feeders seems to peak in late winter and early spring. This is due to decreasing wild food sources, heavy spring snows and early spring migrations. Late March through April is usually the best time to find pine siskins, Cassin's finches, red crossbills, American goldfinches and dark-eyed juncos at your feeders.

Raven.

Birds of the Region

The following section lists the birds that are found in the Denver-Boulder region. This list is not complete. Occasional visitors, uncommon migrants or "rare finds" are generally not included. I have, however, attempted to list all birds that are at least fairly common in our region during some season of the year.

For each bird, the following facts are discussed:

1. *Dates in Area.* Designed to serve as a general guide, indicating when that bird is likely to be found in our region. There will always be early arrivals and late stragglers that do not conform to this schedule.

2. *Local Habitat.* A brief comment regarding the bird's favored habitat within our general area. The habitats include:

PLAINS. Range in elevation from 5000 to approximately 5800 feet, at the base of the foothills. References to lakes, ponds, marshes and grasslands, unless otherwise specified, will imply location on the plains. This varied environment is covered by trips to Barr Lake, Cherry Creek Recreation Area, Chatfield Recreation Area, McClellan Reservoir and Sawhill/Walden Ponds.

LOWER FOOTHILLS (PINYON-JUNIPER ZONE). Extends from the base of the foothills to an elevation of approximately 7000 feet, higher on the south-facing slopes of the foothill canyons. This area is characterized by dry, rocky soil, scrub oak thickets, low shrubs (junipers, mountain mahogany) and scattered rock formations. It is well represented by Red Rocks Park, the South Mesa Trail and the lower section of Waterton Canyon.

Scrub-grassland, Chatfield Reservoir.

Cat-tail marsh, Cherry Creek Reservoir.

UPPER FOOTHILLS (TRANSITION ZONE, "YELLOW PINE ZONE"). Ranges from approximately 6500 to 8000 feet in elevation. It is characterized by open forests of ponderosa pine and Douglas–fir. In the text, Mt. Falcon, Green Mountain Trail and the upper reaches of Waterton and Gregory Canyons have been selected to typify this zone.

MOUNTAIN FORESTS (CANADIAN AND HUDSONIAN ZONES). These dense forests extend from 8000 to 11,500 feet in the higher mountains of the Front Range. Engelmann spruce and lodgepole pines are the primary conifers in this zone. Vast stands of aspen, most abundant from 9000 to 10,000 feet, add to the scenic beauty and diversity. Near timberline, approximately 11,500 feet in our region, the forest thins out and is characterized by stunted spruce, subalpine fir, limber pine and scattered pockets of bristlecone pine. A visit is suggested to the Mt. Evans Area, including Squaw Pass, Chief Mountain, and Echo Lake.

Pinyon-juniper zone, Red Rocks Park.

ALPINE TUNDRA. This treeless, harsh environment extends from timberline to the snow-capped summits of the Front Range. Colorado Route 5, from Echo Lake to the top of Mt. Evans, provides a convenient way to view the birds inhabiting this zone.

3. *Breeding and Wintering Grounds.* One of the most fascinating aspects of birding is the exposure to wild creatures that are often only mere transients in one's home environment. This not only adds to one's understanding of the complexities of nature, but broadens appreciation of the fact that events and policies in distant countries can have a profound impact on the welfare and, indeed, survival of these birds. At the very least, it is interesting to know that the Swainson's hawk, soaring high above you on a summer afternoon, will winter in Argentina, and that the flock of pectoral sandpipers feeding along an area lake are on their way between breeding grounds in arctic Canada and wintering grounds in southern South America.

For these reasons, I have decided to list the general breeding and wintering grounds for each

Transition forest, Green Mountain Trail.

bird. If the bird breeds or winters in our region, the listing is usually omitted.

4. *Comment.* A phrase or two describing unique or characteristic habits of each bird. This is designed to assist with field identification and to broaden the birder's knowledge of the bird's behavior, including its interaction with other species.

5. *Recommendation.* A place and time of year for observing each bird is listed, based on records that I have kept over the past several years. Of course, the reliability of these recommendations will be influenced to some degree by factors such as food crop, water levels and climate variability. However, most birds are quite adaptable and generally adhere to their patterns.

While a given bird may inhabit a local birding area throughout the year, a specific season or month is usually listed to reflect the time that bird is most abundant or conspicuous (due to migrations, breeding behavior, territorial disputes, etc.). For example, Williamson's sapsuckers inhabit certain areas in the Upper Foothills from April through early October. April is recommended since the males arrive at that time of the year and engage in noisy and conspicuous territorial displays.

Aspen-lined meadow in Canadian zone, Squaw Pass Road.

Timberline forest, Mt. Goliath.

Alpine tundra, Mt. Evans.

Loons & Grebes

THE BIRDS

Common Loon
Dates in area: Migrant; April, mid-October to mid-November.
Local habitat: Larger lakes and reservoirs.
Breeding grounds: Canadian lakes.
Wintering grounds: Southern U.S. lakes and coasts.
Comment: Fairly common during fall migration; usually seen alone or in small groups.
Recommendation: McClellan, Barr Lake, Cherry Creek Reservoir; late October.

Arctic Loon
Dates in area: Migrant; April, October-November.
Local habitat: Larger lakes and reservoirs.
Breeding grounds: Arctic Canada and Alaska.
Wintering grounds: Southern Pacific coast of U.S. and Mexico.
Comment: Uncommon migrant in our area but small flocks are regularly seen, especially in fall.
Recommendation: Chatfield, Barr Lake; early November.

Western Grebe
Dates in area: Summer resident; April through mid-November.
Local habitat: Larger lakes and reservoirs.
Wintering grounds: Pacific coast and inland California.
Comment: Our largest grebe; gather in large flocks during migrations; well-known courtship dance is best observed in early May.
Recommendation: Barr Lake, early May; Chatfield, October.

Horned Grebe
Dates in area: Migrant; mid-March to late April, October.

Local habitat: Lakes and reservoirs.
Breeding grounds: Ponds and marshes of northern
U.S. and Canadian prairies.
Wintering grounds: Southern U.S. lakes and coasts.
Comment: Fairly common migrants in our region;
usually seen in small, scattered flocks in the com-
pany of coot and diving ducks.
Recommendation: McClellan Reservoir, mid-April.

Eared Grebe
Dates in area: Primarily a migrant; some breed in
our region; mid-April to early October.
Local habitat: Lakes and reservoirs during migra-
tion; marshes and prairie ponds for breeding.
Breeding grounds: Northern U.S. and Canadian
prairies.
Wintering grounds: Southern U.S. and Central
America.
Comment: Erratic in their presence; best found
during fall migration when they gather in large
flocks.
Recommendation: Barr Lake, late September.

Pied-billed Grebe
Dates in area: Summer resident; April through mid-
November.
Local habitat: Marshes, ponds, shallow lake
margins.
Wintering grounds: Southeastern U.S. and Mexico.
Comment: Common in our region during warmer
months but usually seen alone or in pairs; often
sink below surface when disturbed.
Recommendation: Sawhill Ponds, West Quincy
Lakes; summer.

Pelicans & Cormorants
American White Pelican
Dates in area: Summer resident; May through
October.

Local habitat: Larger lakes and reservoirs.
Breeding grounds: Lakes of northwestern U.S.,
  including northeastern Colorado.
Wintering grounds: Southern coastal areas of U.S.
  and Central America.
Comment: Pelicans in Colorado? Indeed, large
  numbers congregate on reservoirs of northeastern
  Colorado during the summer months. Flocks
  often glide high overhead in mid-afternoon.
Recommendation: Barr Lake, August.

Double-crested Cormorant
Dates in area: Summer resident; April to mid-
  November.
Local habitat: Reservoirs and lakes.
Breeding grounds: Inland lakes of western U.S.
  and Canada, including our region.
Wintering grounds: Southern rivers and coasts of
  U.S. and Mexico.
Comment: These expert fishermen gather in large
  rookeries on area reservoirs during the warm
  months, often in the company of great blue
  herons. After diving for their meal, they typically
  sun themselves on sandbars and tree limbs, with
  wings spread to dry.
Recommendation: Chatfield Reservoir, summer.

Geese & Ducks
Canada Goose
Dates in area: All year; numbers increase in fall
  and winter months.
Local habitat: Rest on lakes, feed in fields, breed in
  marshes.
Breeding grounds: Northern U.S. and Canada,
  including our region.
Wintering grounds: Southern U.S., including our
  area.
Comments: These well-known "honkers" have
  strong family ties and mate for life. They abound
  on area fields and grasslands, including parks

Sawhill/Walden Ponds are magnets for migrating waterfowl.

and golf courses, especially during the colder months.
Recommendation: Barr Lake, Chatfield Reservoir, Cherry Creek Reservoir; late October.

Greater White-fronted Goose
Dates in area: Migrant; April and mid-September to mid-October.
Local habitat: Marshes, lakes and adjacent fields.
Breeding grounds: Arctic Canada.
Wintering grounds: Gulf Coast.
Comment: Migrate earlier in the fall than other geese; while occasionally seen in large flocks, they are more typically found in small groups as they pass through our region.
Recommendation: Sawhill Ponds, Barr Lake; late September through early October.

Mallard
Dates in area: All year.
Local habitat: Marshes, shallow rivers, lake margins.

Breeding grounds: Northern U.S. and Canada,
including our region.
Wintering grounds: Southern U.S. and northern
Mexico, including our region.
Comment: Perhaps our best-known and (in the
west) most abundant wild duck. Usually seen in
pairs or small flocks.
Recommendation: Barr Lake, March.

Northern Pintail
Dates in area: Primarily a migrant; March and
October; smaller numbers in summer and winter.
Local habitat: Shallow lakes, marshes, ponds.
Breeding grounds: Southern U.S. and Mexico.
Comment: These elegant ducks arrive earlier in the
spring than most ducks. Generally gather in
small flocks, often in company of widgeon and
mallards.
Recommendation: Barr Lake, late February to late
March.

Gadwall
Dates in area: Primarily a migrant; March–April
and October; smaller numbers in summer and
winter.
Local habitat: Marshes, ponds, lake margins.
Breeding grounds: Prairie ponds of Northern U.S.
and Canada.
Wintering grounds: Southern U.S. and Mexico.
Comment: These surface-feeders are often found
with coot and widgeon.
Recommendation: West Quincy Lakes, March to
April.

American Widgeon
Dates in area: All year, but most abundant during
migrations, which peak in April and October.
Local habitat: Shallow lakes and ponds.
Breeding grounds: Northern U.S. and Canada.

Wintering grounds: Southern U.S., including our
region if open water is found.
Comment: Gather in huge flocks on area lakes
during migrations, especially in the fall. Widgeon
mingle with coot and diving ducks, from which
they often steal food.
Recommendation: Sawhill Ponds, early October.

Northern Shoveler
Dates in area: Primarily a migrant; April to mid-
May and mid-September to late October.
Local habitat: Shallow lakes and ponds.
Breeding grounds: Northern U.S. and Canada.
Wintering grounds: Southern U.S. and Central
America.
Comment: Generally seen in small flocks; often
gather in shallow ponds where they swim in
circles with heads submerged, feeding on the
plant and animal matter thereby stirred into the
water.
Recommendation: Barr Lake, May.

Blue-winged Teal
Dates in area: Summer resident; mid-April to late
September; most common during migrations,
especially in spring.
Local habitat: Marshes, shallow ponds and
sloughs; flooded fields in spring.
Breeding grounds: Prairie ponds of northern U.S.
and Canada, including northern Colorado.
Wintering grounds: Southern U.S. and Central
America.
Comment: Cinnamon and blue-winged teal move
south earlier (often by late summer) and arrive
later in spring than most other ducks.
Recommendation: Chatfield Reservoir, Barr Lake;
May.

Cinnamon Teal
Dates in area: Summer resident; late April through September.
Local habitat: Marshes, sloughs, shallow ponds.
Breeding grounds: Western U.S.
Wintering grounds: Central America.
Comment: Usually seen in pairs; often mingle with mallards and blue-winged teal; leave for wintering areas by late summer.
Recommendation: West Quincy Lakes, Barr Lake area; May.

Green-winged Teal
Dates in area: Primarily a migrant, peaking in numbers in late March and early November; a fair number winter in our region and a smaller number summer here.
Local habitat: Shallow lakes, marshes, sloughs, flooded fields.
Breeding grounds: Northern U.S. and Canada.
Wintering grounds: Western and southeastern U.S.
Comment: These small but hardy ducks often gather in large flocks during fall migration. However, they typically fly in small, compact groups in rapid, synchronous flight.
Recommendation: Barr Lake, late October; Sawhill Ponds, mid-March.

Wood Duck
Dates in area: Summer resident; March through October; small numbers winter here if open water is found (especially on urban lakes).
Local habitat: Wooded lakes and marshes.
Breeding grounds: Most of U.S. except mountains and the Southwest.
Wintering grounds: Southern U.S. and Pacific coast.
Comment: Females are most often encountered;

frequently seen with ducklings in tow during summer.

Recommendation: Chatfield Reservoir (South Platte marsh), summer.

Redhead

Dates in area: Primarily a migrant; March-April and October-November; small numbers may winter here.

Local habitat: Lakes and reservoirs.

Breeding grounds: Prairie ponds of northern U.S. and Canada.

Wintering grounds: Coastal areas of southern U.S. and Mexico.

Comment: Gather in large flocks on area lakes during migrations. Feed primarily on aquatic plants which they obtain by diving from the surface.

Recommendation: McClellan Reservoir, mid-October; Walden Ponds and West Quincy Lakes, mid-March to mid-April.

Canvasback

Dates in area: Migrant; mid-March to April and late October to early December.

Local habitat: Lakes and reservoirs.

Breeding grounds: Prairie ponds of northern U.S. and Canada.

Wintering grounds: Coastal areas of southern U.S. and Mexico.

Comment: Uncommon; usually seen in pairs or small flocks, mixed with redheads, ring-necked ducks and other divers; generally move south later than other ducks.

Recommendation: West Quincy Lakes, Walden Ponds; late March.

Ring-necked Duck
Dates in area: Migrant; late March to April and
    October–November.
Local habitat: Ponds, lakes and reservoirs.
Breeding grounds: Northern U.S. and Canada.
Wintering grounds: Southern U.S. and Mexico.
Comments: Often gather in large flocks during
    migrations, usually with redheads, lesser scaup
    and coot.
Recommendation: Sawhill Ponds, October;
    McClellan Reservoir, Walden Ponds, mid-April.

Lesser Scaup
Dates in area: Primarily a migrant; mid-March to
    April and late October to November; some
    usually winter here if open water is found.
Local habitat: Lakes and reservoirs.
Breeding grounds: Northern U.S. and Canada.
Wintering grounds: Southern U.S. and Mexico.
Comment: Gather in large flocks on area lakes
    during migrations; usually found feeding with
    redheads, ring-necks and coot.
Recommendation: West Quincy Lakes, McClellan
    Reservoir, late March; Sawhill/Walden Ponds,
    mid-November.

Common Goldeneye
Dates in area: Winter resident; late October to late
    April.
Local habitat: Lakes and reservoirs.
Breeding grounds: Canada and Alaska.
Wintering grounds: Open water throughout most
    of the U.S., including our region.
Comment: These cold-loving ducks are usually seen
    in pairs or small flocks. They are powerful
    divers, feeding on bottom-dwelling plants and
    animals.
Recommendation: Cherry Creek and McClellan

Reservoirs, November to December; McClellan Reservoir and West Quincy Lakes, February to March.

Bufflehead
Dates in area: Winter resident; mid-October to late April.
Local habitat: Lakes, reservoirs and rivers.
Breeding grounds: Canada and Alaska.
Wintering grounds: Open water throughout most of U.S., including our region.
Comment: These small, attractive divers are generally found in scattered flocks, mingled with goldeneyes, mergansers and other diving ducks.
Recommendation: West Quincy Lakes, March to mid-April.

Ruddy Duck
Dates in area: Summer resident; March to November.
Local habitat: Ponds and lake margins.
Breeding grounds: Northern U.S. and Canada, including our region.
Wintering grounds: Coastal areas of southern U.S. and Mexico.
Comment: Despite their small size, ruddy ducks are hardy, being among the first ducks to arrive in the spring and among the last to depart in the fall.
Recommendation: Barr Lake, West Quincy Lakes; October.

Common Merganser
Dates in area: Winter resident; late October to late April.
Local habitat: Lakes, reservoirs and rivers.
Breeding grounds: Mountain lakes and Canada.
Wintering grounds: Open rivers and lakes throughout most of U.S., including our region.
Comment: These streamlined fishermen are most

often seen in small flocks, feeding with gulls and other diving ducks. However, huge flocks are occasionally found on area reservoirs during fall migration.
Recommendation: Cherry Creek Reservoir, mid-November; McClellan Reservoir, February.

Red-breasted Merganser
Dates in area: Migrant; late March to April and mid-October to November; small numbers winter here.
Local habitat: Lakes, reservoirs and rivers.
Breeding grounds: Northern U.S., Canada and Alaska.
Wintering grounds: Coastal areas of southern U.S.
Comment: Uncommon migrants in our region; most often seen in small flocks during fall migration.
Recommendation: Chatfield Reservoir, early November.

Hooded Merganser
Dates in area: Primarily a migrant and winter visitor; late October to April.
Local habitat: Lakes and reservoirs.
Breeding grounds: Northern U.S. and Canada.
Wintering grounds: Southern U.S., including our region if open water remains.
Comment: Fairly common but irregular in their presence during the colder months; usually seen in pairs or small flocks, often in the company of common mergansers and goldeneyes.
Recommendation: McClellan Reservoir, December through February.

Vultures, Hawks, Falcons & Eagles
Turkey Vulture
Dates in area: Summer resident; April to early October.

Local habitat: Foothills, especially along canyons.
Wintering grounds: Southern U.S. and Mexico.
Comment: Usually seen gliding high overhead,
   riding the thermals with a grace that defies their
   reputation. Occasionally seen in groups near
   road-kills and may be encountered in large flocks
   during fall migration.
Recommendation: Waterton Canyon, summer.

Northern Goshawk
Dates in area: All year.
Local habitat: Open conifer forests; higher mountain
   areas in summer, foothills in winter.
Comment: Largest of the Accipiters, goshawks are
   uncommon and generally remain in secluded
   woodlands; feed primarily on grouse.
Recommendation: Green Mountain Trail, winter.

Cooper's Hawk:
Dates in area: Primarily from April to November;
   smaller numbers winter here.
Local habitat: Open forest, especially in the foothills.
Wintering grounds: Southern U.S. and Mexico.
Comment: Best seen near the borders of meadows
   in the foothills, where they hunt for birds and
   rodents.
Recommendation: Mt. Falcon, Gregory Canyon;
   summer.

Sharp-shinned Hawk
Dates in area: All year; numbers peak during
   migrations in April and October.
Local habitat: Open forests of foothills and adjacent
   plains.
Comment: These small Accipiters are usually seen
   as they soar high overhead in the late morning or
   early afternoon. Occasionally seen in large flocks
   during migration. Feed primarily on small birds.

Recommendation: Mt. Falcon, September to
   October.

Northern Harrier (Marsh Hawk)
Dates in area: Primarily April through November;
   most common during migrations; small numbers
   remain through winter.
Local habitat: Grasslands adjacent to wooded
   swamps and lakes.
Wintering grounds: Southern U.S. and Mexico.
Comment: Usually seen perched in wooded
   marshes or flapping low over grasslands, hunting
   for mice.
Recommendation: Cherry Creek Reservoir, mid-
   April to May.

Rough-legged Hawk
Dates in area: Winter resident; late October to
   mid-March.
Local habitat: Grasslands.

Turkey Creek Canyon, bordering Mt. Falcon Park, is a good place for watching the birds of prey that patrol the foothills.

Breeding grounds: Northern Canada and Alaska.
Comment: Fairly common on the plains of eastern Colorado, where they hunt for rodents. Frequently seen hovering above prey.
Recommendation: Barr Lake area, South Mesa Trail; winter.

Ferruginous Hawk
Dates in area: All year; more common during the warmer months.
Local habitat: Grasslands.
Comment: The largest hawks in our region. Hunt for rodents on the prairies and farmlands of eastern Colorado.
Recommendation: Barr Lake area, September to November.

Red-tailed Hawk
Dates in area: All year.
Local habitat: Plains and foothill grasslands.
Comment: Perhaps the most common and best-known buteos in the U.S. Usually seen perched along a highway or near a woods margin, scanning the grassland for rodents.
Recommendation: Barr Lake, Chatfield Reservoir; October to March.

Swainson's Hawk
Dates in area: Summer resident; mid-April to early October.
Local habitat: Grasslands, especially near wooded lakes and streams.
Wintering grounds: South America (primarily Argentina).
Comment: Common on the eastern plains during the warm months. Feed on rodents and large

insects. Often gather in large flocks during
migration.
Recommendation: Barr Lake, May.

Golden Eagle
Dates in area: All year.
Local habitat: Mountain parklands and foothill
canyons.
Comment: These regal hunters are fairly common
in our area throughout the year. Feed primarily
on such mammals as snowshoe hares and
marmots.
Recommendation: Waterton Canyon, summer.

Bald Eagle
Dates in area: Winter resident and visitor; Novem-
ber to mid-April.
Local habitat: Primarily on plains along rivers and
lakeshores; along foothills during migration.
Breeding grounds: Coastal areas of southern Alaska
and British Columbia.
Comment: Our National Birds visit the reservoirs
of eastern Colorado during the winter months.
Recent data suggest that numbers are increasing.
Feed primarily on fish.
Recommendation: Barr Lake (especially near inlet
stream), January.

Osprey
Dates in area: Primarily a migrant, especially in
April and October.
Local habitat: Lakes, reservoirs and rivers.
Wintering grounds: Coastal areas of southern U.S.
and Central America.
Comment: These "fish hawks" are best seen in our
region during spring and fall migrations, when
they stop by to feed on area reservoirs and lakes.
Watching an osprey plunge into the water and

emerge with a fish is truly one of the most
memorable experiences for a birder.
Recommendation: Sawhill Ponds, Cherry Creek
Reservoir, Chatfield; October.

Prairie Falcon
Dates in area: Primarily April to November;
smaller numbers through the winter.
Local habitat: Plains, foothill grasslands; occasion-
ally found above timberline in late summer.
Wintering grounds: Southern plains of U.S. and
Mexico.
Comment: Usually seen darting across your path or
swooping along a ridge in the lower foothills.
Recommendation: Waterton Canyon, South Mesa
Trail; summer.

Merlin (Pigeon Hawk)
Dates in area: All year; numbers increase during
summer.
Local habitat: Open forests of the foothills;
descend to wooded areas on plains during winter.
Comment: Feed on small birds and mice; occasionally wander into residential areas, especially
during colder months, to prey on sparrows and
house finches.
Recommendation: South Mesa Trail, Mt. Falcon;
September to October.

American Kestrel (Sparrow Hawk)
Dates in area: All year; numbers increase during
warmer months.
Local habitat: Plains, foothill grasslands and lower
canyons.
Comment: These small falcons often sit on power
lines along country roads. They feed on grass-
hoppers and mice and are frequently seen
hovering over their prey.

Recommendation: Waterton Canyon, Chatfield
Reservoir; April.

Peregrine Falcon
Dates in area: Primarily a migrant; April and
October–November.
Local habitat: Plains, especially along rivers and
lakes.
Breeding grounds: Arctic Canada and Alaska; re-
introduced in some U.S. cities.
Wintering grounds: Southern U.S. and Central
America.
Comment: Famous for their near-extinction, pere-
grines are making a slow comeback. Formerly
known as duck hawks, they follow and prey on
migrating waterfowl.
Recommendation: Barr Lake, September to October.

Game Birds
Wild Turkey
Dates in area: All year.
Local habitat: Open forests of the foothills.
Comment: Wild turkeys are more common in the
Rampart Range, southwest of Denver, but
scattered flocks may be found in the Denver-
Boulder region. Look for them in forest clearings
during the early evening hours.
Recommendation: Mt. Falcon, September.

Blue Grouse
Dates in area: All year.
Local habitat: Open foothill forests during summer,
conifer forests of higher mountains in winter.
Comment: Usually found alone or in pairs. Forage
along dry, sunny slopes of the foothills during
the warmer months but, paradoxically, ascend to
higher mountain forests when the snows arrive.

Recommendation: Mt. Falcon, Green Mountain Trail; September to October.

White-tailed Ptarmigan
Dates in area: All year.
Local habitat: Open timberline forest and adjacent tundra during warmer months; descend to mountain valleys during the winter.
Comment: These chunky birds are fairly common along the Front Range but tend to localize in limited areas. Due to their protective camouflage they are easily overlooked.
Recommendation: Mt. Evans, July; Guanella Pass, early March.

Guanella Pass provides wintering grounds for a large number of white-tailed ptarmigan.

Ring-necked Pheasant
Dates in area: All year.
Local habitat: Prairie grasslands, farmlands.
Comment: This large Oriental species is locally abundant on the plains of eastern Colorado,

especially in recreation areas where they are not
hunted. Look for them during the colder months,
when the prairie grasses are thinned out and
compressed by snow.
Recommendation: Cherry Creek Recreation Area,
late November.

Egrets, Herons, Ibis & Cranes

Snowy Egret
Dates in area: Summer resident and visitor, May to
mid-September; most numerous in late summer.
Local habitat: Marshes, lake margins.
Wintering grounds: Coastal areas of southern U.S.
and Central America.
Comment: Novice birders and visitors are usually
surprised to find these tropical-looking birds at
the foot of the Rockies. Nevertheless, these
small, active egrets are fairly common in our
region during the summer months.
Recommendation: Barr Lake, August.

Cattle Egret
Dates in area: Summer visitor, especially August to
early September.
Local habitat: Ranchlands, pastures; especially near
lakes and streams; along lakes and reservoirs
during migration.
Wintering grounds: Coastal areas of southeast U.S.
and Mexico.
Comment: These nomads are expanding their range
toward the north and west and will likely
become more common here in the future. Look
for them in late summer, as they gather near area
reservoirs before heading south.
Recommendation: Barr Lake area, early September.

Great Blue Heron
Dates in area: All year, but much more common
from March to September.

Local habitat: Marshes along streams and lakeshores.
Wintering grounds: Southern U.S. and Mexico.
Comment: The "Fishing Long Legs" (from
Michener's *Chesapeake*) breed in large rookeries
along area lakes and reservoirs. They generally
feed alone or in small groups, patiently stalking
their prey at the edge of a stream.
Recommendation: Chatfield Reservoir, summer.

Green-backed Heron
Dates in area: Summer months, especially late
summer.
Local habitat: Marshes, lake margins.
Breeding grounds: Wooded marshes throughout
eastern and central U.S., and along Pacific coast.
Wintering grounds: Gulf coast and coastal areas of
Central America.
Comment: These small herons are primarily visitors
in our region, most common in late summer.
Usually found alone, feeding at the edge of a
marsh or stream.
Recommendation: Sawhill Ponds, August.

Black-crowned Night Heron
Dates in area: Primarily late March to October;
small numbers remain in winter if weather is
mild.
Local habitat: Marshlands along streams and lakes.
Wintering grounds: Along rivers and coastal areas
of southern U.S. and Mexico.
Comment: Breed in large rookeries, one of which is
located in Denver's City Park. Small flocks are
often seen winging their way over Denver on
summer evenings. Look for them during the evening or early morning hours, feeding at marshy
streams or along the South Platte River.
Recommendation: Sawhill Ponds, South Platte
River; summer.

Chatfield's heronry fills with Cormorants and Great Blue Herons during spring and summer.

American Bittern
Dates in area: Late April to early October.
Local habitat: Marshes.
Wintering grounds: Southern U.S. and Mexico.
Comment: These elusive marsh birds are fairly common in our region, though more often heard than seen. Usually found alone; more likely to be seen during early morning or late evening hours.
Recommendation: Sawhill Ponds, Cherry Creek Reservoir, Chatfield Reservoir; August to September.

White-faced Ibis
Dates in area: May to early October; primarily a migrant and summer visitor in our region.
Local habitat: Marshes bordering lakes and reservoirs.
Breeding grounds: Marshlands of northwestern U.S., California, coastal Texas and Mexico.
Wintering grounds: Coastal Texas and Mexico.

Comment: Western counterparts of the glossy ibis, they migrate through our region in large flocks. Most often encountered during spring migration.
Recommendation: Barr Lake, Cherry Creek Reservoir; early May.

Sandhill Crane
Dates in area: Migrant; March to April, October to mid-November.
Local habitat: Marshes, lake margins and adjacent grasslands.
Breeding grounds: Prairie marshes of northern U.S. and Canada.
Wintering grounds: Primarily coastal areas of south Texas and Mexico.
Comment: These birds migrate through our region in large flocks. Most often seen during fall migration, as they stop by to rest on their way to coastal marshes.
Recommendation: Barr Lake, late October.

Rails, Coot & Shorebirds
Virginia Rail
Dates in area: Primarily April to November; some remain through winter if conditions are mild.
Local habitat: Marshes.
Wintering grounds: Gulf coast.
Comment: Like most rails, they usually remain well hidden in the dense marsh vegetation. Look for them during the early morning or late evening hours when they may be found alone feeding at marsh's edge.
Recommendation: Sawhill Ponds, May.

Sora
Dates in area: Summer resident; late April to late September.
Local habitat: Marshes.
Wintering grounds: Gulf coast.

Comment: Best seen at dusk or on cloudy days,
when they may leave the reeds and cattails to
feed along mudflats and streambeds.
Recommendation: Sawhill Ponds, McClellan Reservoir; summer.

American Coot
Dates in area: Primarily March to November; num-
bers increase during migrations and small
numbers linger through the winter if open water
remains.
Local habitat: Marshes and lake margins.
Wintering grounds: Lakes, rivers and coastal
marshes of southern U.S. and Mexico.
Comment: These chunky waterfowl are abundant
on area lakes during spring and fall migrations.
They tend to flock along lake margins, where
they feed in and out of the water.
Recommendation: McClellan Reservoir, April and
October.

Barr Lake's expanding mudflats attract numerous shorebirds in late summer.

American Avocet

Dates in area: Primarily a migrant, especially May and September; small numbers may be found in summer.

Local habitat: Mudflats, shallow marshes, flooded fields.

Breeding grounds: Prairie ponds and marshes of northwestern U.S., including northeastern Colorado.

Wintering grounds: Coastal Texas and Central America.

Comment: These graceful and handsome shorebirds are usually seen in small groups, feeding along mudflats at the border of ponds and lakes.

Recommendation: Chatfield Reservoir, early May; Barr Lake, September.

Mountain Plover

Dates in area: Migrant, especially late March and September.

Local habitat: Grasslands.

Breeding grounds: Short-grass prairie of western U.S., including northeastern Colorado.

Wintering grounds: Central and South America.

Comment: These long-distance travelers are uncommon migrants in the Denver-Boulder area; usually seen in small flocks.

Recommendation: Barr Lake area, September.

Black-bellied Plover

Dates in area: Migrant, especially May and September.

Local habitat: Mudflats, lakeshores, fields.

Breeding grounds: Arctic Canada.

Wintering grounds: Gulf Coast and Pacific coast, from southern U.S. to South America.

Comment: Usually seen alone or in small groups, feeding along area lakes and reservoirs.

Recommendation: Barr Lake area, early May and September.

Semipalmated Plover
Dates in area: Migrant; May and late August to
  early September.
Local habitat: Mudflats, lakeshores.
Breeding grounds: Arctic Canada.
Wintering grounds: Central and South America.
Comment: Generally seen in small flocks, in the
  company of other shorebirds.
Recommendation: Barr Lake, late August.

Killdeer
Dates in area: Primarily March to November; small
  number may winter if conditions are mild.
Local habitat: Mudflats, stream beds, fields.
Wintering grounds: Southern U.S. and Mexico.
Comment: These noisy and conspicuous plovers are
  very common in our region during the warmer
  months. Usually alone or in small groups,
  running and feeding along mudflats that line inlet
  streams of local reservoirs; also common along
  the South Platte river.
Recommendation: Chatfield, Barr Lake, Sawhill
  Ponds; summer.

Long-billed Curlew
Dates in area: Summer resident, April to Septem-
  ber; most common during migrations.
Local habitat: Marsh, prairie ponds, mudflats
  along reservoirs.
Breeding grounds: Western plains of U.S. and
  Canada, including northeastern Colorado.
Wintering grounds: Coastal areas of southern Cali-
  fornia, Texas and Central America.
Comment: These large sandpipers, easily identified
  by their distinctive bills, are uncommon in our
  region. Usually seen alone or in small groups.
Recommendation: Barr Lake area, late August to
  early September.

Marbled Godwit
Dates in area: Migrant; May and August.
Local habitat: Prairie ponds and mudflats along
   lakes.
Breeding grounds: Prairies of northern U.S. and
   Canada.
Wintering grounds: Pacific and Gulf coasts.
Comment: Consistent visitors to our region during
   migrations but numbers vary widely from year to
   year.
Recommendation: Barr Lake, August.

Upland Sandpiper (Upland Plover)
Dates in area: Migrant; April and September.
Local habitat: Prairie grasslands.
Breeding grounds: Prairies of north-central U.S.,
   Canada and Alaska, including northeastern
   Colorado.
Wintering grounds: South America.
Comment: This slender shorebird species used to
   breed in our region; now an uncommon migrant
   here.
Recommendation: Barr Lake, September.

Spotted Sandpiper
Dates in area: Summer resident; mid-April to early
   October.
Local habitat: Along streams, lakeshores and
   marshes.
Wintering grounds: Coastal areas of southern U.S.
   and Central America.
Comment: Common in our region during the
   warmer months but usually seen alone or in
   pairs, bobbing along rocky streams or lakeshores.
Recommendation: Sawhill Ponds, summer.

Solitary Sandpiper
Dates in area: Migrant; early May and late August
   to September.

Local habitat: Along streams, ponds and lake-
   shores; occasionally feed in flooded fields.
Breeding grounds: Northern Canada and Alaska.
Wintering grounds: Central and South America.
Comment: These long-distance migrants are un-
   common in our region and, like spotted sand-
   pipers, are usually found alone.
Recommendation: Barr Lake, September.

Willet
Dates in area: Migrant; May and September.
Local habitat: Mudflats and sandbars along streams
   and lakeshores.
Breeding grounds: Prairies of northern U.S. and
   Canada.
Wintering grounds: Pacific and Gulf coasts.
Comment: These large sandpipers are regular but
   uncommon migrants in our region; usually seen
   in small groups.
Recommendation: Cherry Creek Reservoir, Barr
   Lake; early May.

Yellowlegs (Greater and *Lesser)*
Dates in area: Migrants; April and late August to
   October.
Local habitat: Marshes, mudflats.
Breeding grounds: Northern Canada and Alaska.
Wintering grounds: Gulf coast of U.S. and Central
   America.
Comment: Lesser yellowlegs are occasionally seen
   in large flocks, but both species are more often
   found in small groups. Fall migrants begin to
   arrive by late August and some may yet be seen
   here in late October.
Recommendation: Sawhill Ponds, Barr Lake; late
   September to October.

Stilt Sandpiper
Dates in area: Migrant; May and late August to
   mid-September.

Local habitat: Mudflats, lakeshores.
Breeding grounds: Arctic Canada.
Wintering grounds: South America.
Comment: These slender shorebirds are regular but uncommon migrants in our region. Usually seen in small groups, feeding along lakeshores with other sandpipers.
Recommendation: Barr Lake, late August.

Long-billed Dowitcher
Dates in area: Migrant; April and mid-September to October.
Local habitat: Mudflats, sandbars, lakeshores.
Breeding grounds: Coastal areas of Alaska.
Wintering grounds: Pacific and Gulf coasts.
Comment: Common migrants in our region; often seen in large flocks, especially in the fall. Feed along shallow lake margins.
Recommendation: Barr Lake, October.

Pectoral Sandpiper
Dates in area: Migrant; April and September.
Local habitat: Lakeshores, flooded fields.
Breeding grounds: Arctic Canada and Alaska.
Wintering grounds: Southern South America.
Comment: These long-distance travelers are regular but uncommon migrants in our region; usually seen in small flocks.
Recommendation: Barr Lake, September.

Baird's Sandpiper
Dates in area: Migrant; April and September.
Local habitat: Mudflats, lakeshores, flooded fields.
Breeding grounds: Arctic Canada.
Wintering grounds: South America.
Comment: These medium-sized shorebirds are often abundant along area lakes during the fall

migration. Like pectoral sandpipers, they favor
moist, grassy areas.
Recommendation: Barr Lake, September.

Least Sandpiper
Dates in area: Migrant; May and August–September.
Local habitat: Mudflats and flooded fields.
Breeding grounds: Canada and Alaska.
Wintering grounds: Gulf and Pacific coasts of
   southern U.S. and Central America.
Comment: Smallest of the sandpipers, these "peeps"
   usually migrate through in large flocks. Feed in
   grassy areas that border lakes and ponds.
Recommendation: Barr Lake, September.

Semipalmated Sandpiper
Dates in area: Migrant; especially May and late
   August.
Local habitat: Mudflats lining streams and lakes.
Breeding grounds: Arctic Canada and Alaska.
Wintering grounds: Gulf Coast of Central and
   South America.
Comment: These shorebirds migrate in large flocks
   and are among the earliest of the fall migrants,
   often arriving by late July.
Recommendation: Barr Lake, late August.

Western Sandpiper
Dates in area: Migrant; April and August–September.
Local habitat: Mudflats, shallow lake margins,
   flooded fields.
Wintering grounds: Pacific and Gulf coasts of
   southern U.S. and Central America.
Comment: These shorebirds are usually seen in
   large flocks, probing for food in the shallow
   waters of area lakes and reservoirs.
Recommendation: Barr Lake, August.

Sanderling
Dates in area: Migrant; especially early May and
late August to early September.
Local habitat: Mudflats and lakeshores.
Breeding grounds: Arctic Canada.
Wintering grounds: Coasts of southern U.S. and
Central America.
Comment: These sandpipers are usually seen in
small flocks, feeding along mudflats that border
lakes. They are very active birds, roaming
constantly as they feed.
Recommendation: Barr Lake, early September.

Wilson's Phalarope
Dates in area: Migrant; especially early May and
late September.
Local habitat: Flooded fields, lake margins and
prairie ponds.
Breeding grounds: Prairie ponds of northern U.S.
and Canada.
Wintering grounds: South America.
Comment: Large flocks move through our area
during migrations, especially in the spring. They
favor shallow waters, in which they spin to stir
food matter to the surface.
Recommendation: Barr Lake (especially flooded
fields in area), early May.

Northern Phalarope
Dates in area: Migrant; May, September–October.
Local habitat: Shallow lake margins.
Breeding grounds: Northern Canada.
Wintering grounds: Winter at sea.
Comment: Much less common in our region than
are the Wilson's phalaropes. Nevertheless, they
are regularly seen here in small flocks, especially
during fall migration.
Recommendation: Chatfield Reservoir, Barr Lake;
early October.

Common Snipe
Dates in area: All year; numbers increase during the warmer months.
Local habitat: Marshes and dense vegetation along streams.
Wintering grounds: Southern U.S. and Mexico, including our region.
Comment: These common but elusive birds are usually found when accidentally flushed from stream beds. Though snipes look like birds that should fly to southern coasts for the winter, a fair number can be found here during the cold months.
Recommendation: Cherry Creek Reservoir (see text), February to April.

Gulls & Terns

Herring Gull
Dates in area: Winter visitor; November to early April.
Local habitat: Lakes, reservoirs and South Platte River.
Breeding grounds: Alaska, Canada and north-central U.S.
Wintering grounds: Along rivers and coasts of southern U.S.
Comment: Though abundant in many areas of the U.S. (especially along the Great Lakes and East Coast), herring gulls visit our area only in small flocks, during the colder months. Most often seen in late fall.
Recommendation: McClellan Reservoir, December.

California Gull
Dates in area: Summer resident; mid-April to mid-November.
Local habitat: Prairies, near lakes and reservoirs.
Breeding grounds: Prairie lakes of northwestern U.S. and Canada, including northeastern Colorado.

Wintering grounds: Pacific Coast.

Comment: Like most gulls and terns, these birds are colonial, nesting and feeding in large flocks. Often seen in cultivated fields feeding on grasshoppers and other insects.

Recommendation: Barr Lake area, late September to October.

Ring-billed Gull

Dates in area: All year.

Local habitat: Lakes, reservoirs and along South Platte River.

Comment: These gulls are very common on area lakes and reservoirs throughout the year. They frequently scavange for food at shopping centers, especially in winter.

Recommendation: McClellan Reservoir, February.

Franklin's Gull

Dates in area: May to early November.

Local habitat: Prairies, near lakes and reservoirs.

Breeding grounds: Northern U.S. and Canada, including northeastern Colorado.

Wintering grounds: Gulf and Pacific coasts of Central and South America.

Comment: These small gulls are abundant in our region during fall migration. Often seen roaming over the city on late summer evenings, feeding on insects.

Recommendation: Barr Lake, October.

Forster's Tern

Dates in area: Primarily a migrant; especially late April and early September; small numbers summer here.

Local habitat: Prairie marshes and lakes.

Breeding grounds: Prairie marshes of northern U.S. and Canada.

Wintering grounds: Gulf and Pacific coasts of
  southern U.S. and Central America.
Comment: Regular but uncommon migrants in our
  region. Best identified during fall migration,
  when winter plummage is present.
Recommendation: Barr Lake, early September.

Black Tern
Dates in area: Primarily a migrant; especially late
  May and early September.
Local habitat: Prairie lakes and marshes.
Breeding grounds: Prairie marshes of northern U.S.
  and Canada.
Wintering grounds: South America.
Comment: These distinctive terns are often seen in
  large flocks, especially during spring migration.
  They resemble Franklin's gulls in their habits,
  roaming over marshes and fields in search of flying
  insects.
Recommendation: Barr Lake, late May.

Doves & Cuckoos

Rock Dove
Dates in area: All year.
Local habitat: Everywhere! These well-known birds
  have adapted to a myriad of urban and rural
  habitats, roosting under bridges and eaves, and
  feeding on lawns and fields.
Comment: Known to most as the "city pigeon,"
  these opportunists also breed along the lower
  foothills. A large flock has settled in at Red
  Rocks Park, roosting in small caverns and
  crevices in the sandstone.
Recommendation: Red Rocks Park, all year (some-
  how they seem more natural here).

Band-tailed Pigeon
Dates in area: Summer resident and visitor; late
  May to early October.

Local habitat: Open woodlands of lower foothills.

Wintering grounds: Southwestern U.S. and Mexico.

Comment: These birds are best found in late summer, when they usually gather in large flocks, feeding and roosting on the sunny slopes of foothill canyons.

Recommendation: Mt. Falcon, mid-September.

Mourning Dove

Dates in area: Primarily mid-April to early November; small number may remain through the winter.

Local habitat: Residential areas, farmlands, grasslands.

Wintering grounds: Southern U.S. and Mexico.

Comment: This bird's "mournful" song is a welcome sound after a long, cold winter. Most often seen sitting on wires along alleys and country roads, but may be found in large flocks feeding on prairie grasslands.

Recommendation: Residential areas, summer.

Yellow-billed Cuckoo

Dates in area: Summer resident and visitor; June to September.

Local habitat: Wooded areas along streams of the plains and lower foothills.

Breeding grounds: Most of the U.S. except high mountain areas.

Wintering grounds: South America.

Comment: Uncommon residents in our region during the warmer months. Favor moist woodlands and feed primarily on caterpillars.

Recommendation: Chatfield, lower Waterton Canyon; early summer.

Owls

Screech Owl

Dates in area: All year.

Local habitat: Woodlots, especially cottonwoods,
along streams, lakes and marshes; plains and
lower foothills.
Comment: This species is the most common small
owl throughout most of the U.S. Often found
resting in a tree cavity.
Recommendation: Barr Lake, all year (especially
winter).

Great Horned Owl
Dates in area: All year.
Local habitat: Wooded marshlands; hunt on
adjacent grasslands.
Comment: The largest owls in our region. They
nest very early in the year and their downy
young may be seen peering from the nest by late
March. Feed on rodents and other small mammals.
Recommendation: Chatfield and Cherry Creek
Recreation areas, all year.

Long-eared Owl
Dates in area: All year; more common during
colder months.
Local habitat: Wooded marshes and lake margins
on plains; wooded ravines in foothills.
Comment: Unlike most owls, this species often
roosts in groups, especially during the winter.
Much less common than great horned owl in our
region.
Recommendation: Barr Lake, winter.

Short-eared Owl
Dates in area: Winter resident and visitor; November to April.
Local habitat: Marshes and grasslands along lakes.
Breeding grounds: Northern U.S., Canada and
Alaska.
Comment: Often active during the day. They
resemble the northern harrier as they flap low
over a marsh, hunting for rodents.

Great horned owls are best found in cottonwood groves along streams and marshes.

Recommendation: Barr Lake, Cherry Creek Reservoir; winter.

Burrowing Owl
Dates in area: Primarily April to October; small number may linger through winter.
Local habitat: Prairie grasslands.
Wintering grounds: Southwestern U.S.
Comment: These small owls nest in abandoned prairie dog burrows. Often seen standing next to the burrow, intermittently pouncing on grasshoppers.
Recommendation: Chatfield Reservoir (at prairie dog town), summer.

Northern Saw-whet Owl
Dates in area: All year; more common during colder months.

Local habitat: Conifer forests of mountains and
foothills.
Comment: Fairly common in our region, but hunts
at night and is rarely seen. Look for them
roosting in a cluster of small ponderosa pines.
Recommendation: Gregory Canyon, winter.

Northern Pygmy Owl
Dates in area: All year.
Local habitat: Conifer forests of mountains and
foothills.
Comment: Another small owl species that is more
common in our mountain forests than the birder
might appreciate. They are occasionally active
during the day and may be seen hunting for mice.
Recommendation: Mt. Evans Area, all year
(especially winter); Gregory Canyon, winter.

Goatsuckers & Swifts
Common Poor-will
Dates in area: Summer resident; late April to
September.
Local habitat: Open woodlands and meadows of
lower foothills.
Wintering grounds: Southwestern U.S. and Central
America.
Comment: Their mellow calls echo across the foot-
hill grasslands on summer evenings. However,
poor-wills are rarely seen, unless accidentally
flushed from their cover.
Recommendation: Red Rocks Park, South Mesa
Trail; summer.

Common Nighthawk
Dates in area: Summer resident; June to September.
Local habitat: Open woodlands of plains and lower
foothills; also nests on rooftops in urban areas.
Wintering grounds: South America.
Comment: Most often seen on calm summer

evenings, flying above the city, feeding on insects; often seen in the company of Franklin's gulls.
Recommendation: Over Metro Denver evenings, late August to early September.

White-throated Swift
Dates in area: Summer resident; late April to early September.
Local habitat: Canyons and cliffs along foothills.
Wintering grounds: Southwestern U.S. and Central America.
Comment: These "flying cigars" feed in noisy flocks, often in the company of cliff and violet-green swallows. Nest on rocky canyon walls.
Recommendation: Red Rocks Park, summer.

Hummingbirds
Broad-tailed Hummingbird
Dates in area: Summer resident; late May to early September.
Local habitat: Moist ravines of the foothill forests.
Wintering grounds: Central America.
Comment: Often encountered in residential areas during migrations.
Recommendation: Gregory Canyon, summer.

Kingfishers
Belted Kingfisher
Dates in area: All year; numbers increase during warmer months.
Local habitat: Along streams, wooded marshes and lakeshores.
Comment: These birds' distinctive, rattling call frequently heralds their presence. Almost always seen alone or in pairs, perched on a dead snag or winging their way along a stream.
Recommendation: Chatfield (South Platte marsh), summer.

Woodpeckers

Northern Flicker (Red-Shafted Flicker)
Dates in area: All year.
Local habitat: Residential areas, woodlots on
plains, and open woodlands of foothills.
Comment: Largest and most common woodpecker
in local residential areas. Often gather in flocks
and feed on ground-dwelling insects. Attracted to
suet feeders in winter.
Recommendation: Highline Canal, residential
areas; all year.

Red-headed Woodpecker
Dates in area: Summer resident, mid-May to mid-
September.
Local habitat: Open woodlands of plains and lower
foothills.
Wintering grounds: Southeastern U.S.

*Backwater marshes are
a favored habitat of the
belted kingfisher.*

Comment: This attractive, eastern woodpecker is expanding its range westward. Often found in wooded marshes, where dead trees provide food and shelter.
Recommendation: Barr Lake (see text), summer.

Lewis' Woodpecker
Dates in area: All year.
Local habitat: Open woodlands in foothills and wooded streams on plains; numbers increase on plains during colder months.
Comment: This woodpecker is fairly common but locally concentrated in our region. Like flickers, Lewis' woodpeckers often gather in flocks.
Recommendation: Lower Waterton Canyon, Chatfield (along South Platte); all year (especially colder months).

Williamson's Sapsucker
Dates in area: Summer resident; April to early October.
Local habitat: Upper foothills (Transition Zone forests).
Wintering grounds: Southwestern U.S. and Mexico.
Comment: These flashy woodpeckers are common in our region, but tend to localize in certain areas. They favor open forest of Douglas–fir and ponderosa pine. Listen for their distinctive, stuttered drumming in mid-April.
Recommendation: Green Mountain Trail, mid-April.

Yellow-bellied Sapsucker
Dates in area: Summer resident; April to mid-October.
Local habitat: Mountain forests, especially aspen groves; woodlots on plains during migrations.
Wintering grounds: Southern U.S. and Central America.
Comment: As their name implies, these woodpeckers

Woodpecker heaven, Green Mountain Trail.

feed on sap that oozes from the holes they drill.
Usually found alone.
Recommendation: Mt. Evans area (see text),
summer.

Hairy Woodpecker
Dates in area: All year.
Local habitat: Favor open woodlands of upper
foothills, but may be found from woodlots on
plains to timberline. Much less common in resi-
dential areas than the similar downy woodpeckers.
Comment: Less conspicuous than flickers and
Williamson's sapsuckers, hairy woodpeckers are
nevertheless common in the open Transition
Zone forests of the upper foothills. Often seen
hammering away at yucca stalks or fallen trees.
Recommendation: Mt. Falcon, Green Mountain

Trail; all year (especially late March through April).

Downy Woodpecker
Dates in area: All year.
Local habitat: Foothill forests and woodlots on plains.
Comment: Our smallest woodpecker. Downies frequently roam through residential areas, especially during colder months. Often turn up at suet feeders.
Recommendation: Chatfield, Barr Lake; all year (especially winter).

Three-toed Woodpecker
Dates in area: All year.
Local habitat: Conifer forests of mountains; may descend to foothills during winter.
Comment: This mountain resident is fairly common in the high forests of the Front Range but generally favors dense habitat and is seldom seen by the casual visitor.
Recommendation: Mt. Evans area, summer.

Kingbirds & Flycatchers
Eastern Kingbird
Dates in area: Summer resident; May to mid-September.
Local habitat: Wooded marshes and adjacent grass-lands.
Wintering grounds: South America.
Comment: These large, noisy flycatchers are usually found alone during the spring but by late summer have gathered in flocks, often in the company of western flycatchers.
Recommendation: Chatfield (South Platte marsh), summer.

Western Kingbird
Dates in area: Summer resident; May to September.
Local habitat: Grasslands, especially near lakes and
  woods margins.
Wintering grounds: Central and South America.
Comment: Generally found in small flocks,
  flycatching from power lines or dead tree snags;
  gather in large flocks by late summer.
Recommendation: Barr Lake, Highline Canal; late
  summer.

Say's Phoebe
Dates in area: Summer resident; mid-April to late
  September.
Local habitat: Foothill grasslands, farmlands;
  occasionally on alpine meadows (late summer).
Wintering grounds: Southwestern U.S. and Central
  America.
Comment: These birds are common in our region
  but tend to concentrate in limited areas. Unlike
  most flycatchers, they favor the open, semi-arid
  country that characterizes the lower foothills and
  adjacent plains.
Recommendation: Lower Waterton Canyon, Red
  Rocks Park, South Mesa Trail; summer.

Hammond's Flycatcher
Dates in area: Summer resident; May to September.
Local habitat: Conifer forests of mountains and
  foothills.
Wintering grounds: South America.
Comment: This small flycatcher breeds in open
  mountain forests and is often found as high as
  timberline.
Recommendation: Mt. Evans area (especially Mt.
  Goliath; see text), summer.

Dusky Flycatcher
Dates in area: Summer resident; May to September.

Local habitat: Open forests of mountains and
foothills.
Wintering grounds: Central America.
Comment: Another small, high-altitude flycatcher.
They favor open, sunny areas and are thus
usually found along mountain meadows.
Recommendation: Gregory Canyon, summer.

Western Flycatcher
Dates in area: Summer resident; May to September.
Local habitat: Foothill forests, especially along
streams.
Wintering grounds: Central America.
Comment: Favor moist ravines and are most com-
mon in wooded canyons of the foothills.
Recommendation: Gregory Canyon, summer.

Western Wood Pewee
Dates in area: Summer resident; May to September.
Local habitat: Wooded streams of foothills and
plains; mountain forests.
Wintering grounds: South America.
Comment: Most often seen hunting along open
woodlands that border the streams and lakes of
the plains and lower foothills.
Recommendation: Barr Lake, May; Gregory
Canyon, summer.

Olive-sided Flycatcher
Dates in area: Summer resident; mid-May to mid-
September.
Local habitat: Open forests of mountains and foot-
hills; along wooded streams on plains during
migrations.
Wintering grounds: South America.
Comment: Usually found near forest clearings,
singing or hunting from a dead branch. Three-
note call is distinctive.

Recommendation: Green Mountain Trail, June;
Mt. Evans area (near timberline), summer.

Larks
Horned Lark
Dates in area: All year; numbers increase during
fall and winter months.
Local habitat: Prairie grasslands; may be found on
alpine meadows or tundra in late summer.
Comment: Large flocks of horned larks roam the
plains of eastern Colorado during the colder
months. They often feed along country roads and
burst into the air as your car approaches.
Recommendation: Chatfield, Barr Lake; winter.

Swallows
Barn Swallow
Dates in area: Summer resident; late April to mid-
October.
Local habitat: Along streams, culverts and lakes on
the plains; also in lower foothill canyons.
Wintering grounds: South America.
Comment: Commonly seen in large flocks, resting
on power lines or swooping over waterways,
feeding on insects.
Recommendation: Lower Waterton Canyon,
summer.

Cliff Swallow
Dates in area: Summer resident; late April to
September.
Local habitat: Foothill canyons and ravines.
Wintering grounds: South America.
Comment: These swallows are very common along
the lower foothills, feeding in large flocks, often
in the company of white-throated swifts.

Recommendation: Lower Waterton Canyon, Red Rocks Park; summer.

Violet-green Swallow
Dates in area: Summer resident; May to mid-September.
Local habitat: Canyons of mountains and foothills.
Wintering grounds: Central and South America.
Comment: These swallows seem to favor higher elevations than the other species; may be seen as high as timberline.
Recommendation: Waterton Canyon, Green Mountain Trail; June.

Tree Swallow
Dates in area: Summer resident; April to September.
Local habitat: Along streams and lakes on the plains and in foothill canyons.
Wintering grounds: Southern U.S. and Central America.
Comment: These gregarious birds are often abundant along lakeshores and marshy streams during migrations. As their name implies they nest in tree cavities.
Recommendation: Chatfield, Barr Lake; summer.

Rough-winged Swallow
Dates in area: Summer resident; April to September.
Local habitat: Along streams, lakes and marshes on the plains.
Wintering grounds: Central and South America.
Comment: Unlike the other swallows, they are most often seen in small groups; generally feed along marshy streams and rest on power lines.
Recommendation: Sawhill Ponds, Barr Lake; summer.

Jays, Magpies & Nutcrackers

Blue Jay
Dates in area: All year.
Local habitat: Residential areas of plains and lower
    foothills.
Comment: These well-known, eastern jays are ex-
    panding their range westward. Noisy and aggres-
    sive, they tend to dominate other birds at feeders.
Recommendation: Backyard; seem most
    conspicuous in spring and late summer.

Steller's Jay
Dates in area: All year.
Local habitat: Open forests of mountains and foot-
    hills.
Comment: Usually abundant in the open pine
    forest of the Transition Zone. Replace blue jays
    in the higher elevations of the West.
Recommendation: Mt. Falcon, South Mesa Trail;
    all year.

Scrub Jay
Dates in area: All year.
Local habitat: Dry, lower foothills (Pinyon-Juniper
    Zone).
Comment: Common in the scrub-oak country of
    the lower foothills. Tend to remain hidden in
    thickets feeding on or near the ground. Often
    alight on boulders to survey the area.
Recommendation: Red Rocks Park, Lower Water-
    ton Canyon; all year.

Gray Jay
Dates in area: All year.
Local habitat: Conifer forests of mountains; some
    descend to foothills in winter.

Comment: Well-known around ski areas and
mountain picnic grounds, where they turn up for
handouts.
Recommendation: Mt. Evans area, all year.

Black-billed Magpie
Dates in area: All year.
Local habitat: Favors grasslands with scattered
trees; plains and foothills.
Comment: These well-known, flashy birds are
omnivorous, feeding on small mammals, insects,
berries, waste grain and carrion. Often seen on
the backs of deer and cattle, looking for ticks.
Their huge nests of sticks are frequently used in
later years by great horned owls.
Recommendation: Chatfield and Cherry Creek
Recreation Areas; all year.

Clarke's Nutcracker
Dates in area: All year.
Local habitat: Mountain forests, especially near
timberline; occasionally descend to foothills and
adjacent plains in winter.
Comment: Like the gray jays, these attractive birds
are well-known to those who journey into the
mountain back-country, since they often drop by
for handouts. Otherwise they feed primarily on
conifer seeds, insects and berries.
Recommendation: Mt. Evans area, all year.

Ravens & Crows
Common Raven
Dates in area: All year.
Local habitat: Open forests and tundra, especially
along cliffs and canyons; in high mountains all
year; some descend into foothills during the
winter.
Comment: These large, hardy scavengers roam the

high mountain ridges throughout the year. Often seen feasting on roadkills during the colder months.

Recommendation: Squaw Pass Road, all year; Green Mountain Trail, winter.

American Crow

Dates in area: All year.

Local habitat: Plains and foothill grasslands.

Comment: These infamous and gregarious birds are usually heard before they are seen. They are omnivorous and frequently invade residential areas, especially during the colder months.

Recommendation: Chatfield and Cherry Creek Reservoirs; late summer and fall.

Chickadees, Bushtits & Nuthatches

Black-capped Chickadee

Dates in area: All year.

Local habitat: Foothill forests and woodlots on the plains, especially along streams.

Comment: This is the common chickadee of the plains and lower foothills. Often abundant in small trees lining streams and lake shores. Common at backyard feeders during the winter.

Recommendation: Chatfield, Barr Lake; all year (especially colder months).

Mountain Chickadee

Dates in area: All year.

Local habitat: Conifer forests of mountains and foothills; may wander onto plains during the colder months.

Comment: These small birds move about the mountain forests in large flocks, often feeding with nuthatches.

Recommendation: Mt. Evans area, summer; Green Mountain Trail, South Mesa Trail, fall and winter.

Bushtit
Dates in area: Winter visitor (irregular).
Local habitat: Lower foothills (Pinyon-Juniper Zone).
Breeding grounds: Southwestern U.S., including southern Colorado.
Comment: These tiny birds roam about in large flocks during the winter months. Their presence in our region is erratic and unpredictable.
Recommendation: Waterton Canyon, Shadow Canyon; late winter.

White-breasted Nuthatch
Dates in area: All year.
Local habitat: Mountain and foothill forests; woodlots on plains.
Comment: Largest of the nuthatches. Usually seen alone or in pairs. More common in deciduous woodlands than are the other nuthatches.
Recommendation: Mt. Falcon, Green Mountain Trail; March and April.

Red-breasted Nuthatch
Dates in area: All year.
Local habitat: Conifer forests of mountains and foothills; often descend onto plains during colder months.
Comment: Usually found alone or in pairs, but they feed with mountain chickadees. Fairly common at backyard feeders during the winter, especially if large conifers are nearby.
Recommendation: South Mesa Trail, Gregory Canyon; September.

Pygmy Nuthatch
Dates in area: All year.
Local habitat: Conifer forests of mountains and foothills, especially in ponderosa pines of the

Transition Zone; may wander onto plains in winter.

Comment: Unlike other nuthatches, these birds usually move about in large flocks.

Recommendation: Green Mountain Trail, early October through November.

Brown Creeper

Dates in area: All year.

Local habitat: Conifer forests of mountains and foothills; woodlots on plains during colder months.

Comment: Usually found alone. Feed on insects or larvae that reside and hibernate in tree bark. Fairly common in residential areas during late fall and winter.

Recommendation: Green Mountain Trail, October and November; Chatfield, winter.

Dippers

Dipper

Dates in area: All year.

Local habitat: Mountain streams; descend to foothill canyons and occasionally onto plains during colder months.

Comment: These magicians of the bird world actually submerge in white-water streams to feed on insects and larvae.

Recommendation: Waterton Canyon, November through April.

Wrens

House Wren

Dates in area: Summer resident; May to September.

Local habitat: Wooded areas along streams, marshes and lakes; residential areas.

Wintering grounds: Southern U.S. and Central America.

Comment: These small, noisy and very active birds are often abundant in the groves of cottonwoods lining area streams.

Recommendation: Highline Canal, summer.

Rock Wren

Dates in area: Summer resident; late April to early October.

Local habitat: Along canyons and rock formations of the lower foothills.

Wintering grounds: Southwestern U.S. and Central America.

Comment: Usually found alone or in small groups, bobbing along boulder fields and rock slides of the Pinyon-Juniper Zone.

Recommendation: South Mesa Trail, late summer.

Canyon Wren

Dates in area: All year.

Local habitat: Foothill canyons.

Comment: Usually found alone; has a distinctive, cascade-like call. Does not migrate (unlike rock wren).

Recommendation: Gregory Canyon, Waterton Canyon; all year.

Marsh Wren (Long-billed Marsh Wren)

Dates in area: All year; numbers increase during warmer months.

Local habitat: Cattail marshes along ponds and lakes.

Wintering grounds: Southern U.S. and Mexico.

Comment: This timid marsh resident is usually found alone or in pairs. Best seen at dawn or dusk.

Recommendation: Sawhill Ponds, summer.

Thrushes, Bluebirds & Pipits

Northern Mockingbird
Dates in area: Summer resident and visitor; late
    April to late September.
Local habitat: Open woodlands of the plains,
    especially near lakes and reservoirs.
Wintering grounds: Southern U.S.
Comment: This eastern bird is extending its range
    westward but is still uncommon in our region.
Recommendation: Barr Lake, May.

Gray Catbird
Dates in area: Summer resident; May to September.
Local habitat: Thickets along streams of the plains
    and lower foothills.
Wintering grounds: Gulf coastal areas of southern
    U.S. and Central America.

*Like these bighorn
sheep, canyon and rock
wrens favor the dry,
sunny slopes of
Waterton Canyon.*

Comment: These noisy birds are especially common along moist ravines of the lower foothills.
Recommendation: Waterton Canyon, June.

Brown Thrasher
Dates in area: Summer resident and visitor; May to September.
Local habitat: Thickets along lakes, streams and wood margins of plains and lower foothills.
Wintering grounds: Southeastern U.S.
Comment: Uncommon in our region. Scratches and feeds on the ground as towhees do.
Recommendation: Barr Lake, May.

American Robin
Dates in area: All year.
Local habitat: Residential areas, parks, fields, foothill grasslands; even on tundra in late summer.
Comment: No introduction needed! To convince yourself that not all robins head south for the winter, visit Red Rocks Park in January; a large flock winters here, feeding on berries.
Recommendation: Red Rocks Park, winter months.

Townsend's Solitaire
Dates in area: All year.
Local habitat: Open mountain forests in summer; foothill canyons in winter.
Comment: These birds are "not-so-solitary" during the fall and winter months, when they gather in large flocks along wooded ravines of the foothills. They look like robins but act like flycatchers.
Recommendation: Red Rocks Park; winter.

Hermit Thrush
Dates in area: Summer resident; early May to October.
Local habitat: Mountain forests; migrant on plains.

Wintering grounds: Southern U.S. and Central America.
Comment: Like most thrushes, this bird feeds on ground-dwelling insects, worms and berries; thus is usually in low thickets or on the ground. Perhaps best found during migration.
Recommendation: Barr Lake, May; Mt. Evans area, summer.

Veery
Dates in area: Summer resident; May to September.
Local habitat: Mountain forests; migrant on plains.
Wintering grounds: South America.
Comment: This small thrush favors moist areas and is thus best found along mountain streams.
Recommendation: Mt. Evans area, summer.

Swainson's Thrush
Dates in area: Migrant; especially May and late September.
Local habitat: Wooded areas on plains, especially along streams and lakes.
Breeding grounds: Northwestern U.S. and Canada.
Wintering grounds: South America.
Comment: These birds are fairly common in our region during migrations, when they may appear in large flocks.
Recommendation: Barr Lake, early May.

Western Bluebird
Dates in area: Summer resident; April to October.
Local habitat: Semi-open country, especially in the foothills.
Wintering grounds: Southwestern U.S. and Mexico.
Comment: These colorful birds often gather in large flocks during the late summer and early fall, feeding on insects and berries, favoring wooded meadows of the foothills.

Bluebird country, Green Mountain Trail.

Recommendation: Mt. Falcon, Green Mountain Trail; September to mid-October.

Mountain Bluebird
Dates in area: All year but primarily March to October.
Local habitat: Mountain meadows, including tundra in late summer; move onto plains in winter.
Comment: These attractive birds are usually seen in pairs or small groups but often mingle with flocks of western bluebirds in late summer.
Recommendation: Mt. Evans area (see text), summer; Mt. Falcon, Green Mountain Trail, September to mid-October.

Water Pipit
Dates in area: Summer resident; mid-April to
    October; small numbers may winter here.
Local habitat: Tundra during summer; open fields
    on plains during migration.
Wintering grounds: Southern U.S. and Central
    America.
Comment: These birds are common along alpine
    lakes during the warmer months and are occa-
    sionally seen in large flocks during migrations.
Recommendation: Mt. Evans, especially along
    Summit Lake; July.

Kinglets

Golden-crowned Kinglet
Dates in area: All year.
Local habitat: Conifer forests of mountains and
    foothills; may descend onto plains in winter.
Comment: Despite their small size, these birds are
    very hardy and generally remain in the mountain
    forests throughout the year.
Recommendation: Mt. Evans area, summer.

Ruby-crowned Kinglet
Dates in area: Primarily April to mid-October;
    small numbers may remain through winter.
Local habitat: Conifer forests of mountains and
    foothills; woodlots on plains during migration.
Wintering grounds: Southern U.S. and Mexico.
Comment: These small birds, like the warblers they
    resemble, are very active feeders. Often flock
    together with mountain chickadees and
    nuthatches.
Recommendation: Mt. Evans area (see text),
    summer.

Waxwings

Bohemian Waxwing
Dates in area: Winter visitors.

Local habitat: Semi-open country of foothills and
plains.
Breeding grounds: Western Canada and Alaska.
Wintering grounds: Northwestern U.S., including
our region.
Comment: Like other waxwings, these birds roam
about in large flocks during the colder months.
Their presence is erratic and unpredictable.
Recommendation: Residential areas, Red Rocks
Park, Shadow Canyon; winter.

Cedar Waxwing
Dates in area: All year; erratic.
Local habitat: Semi-open country of foothills and
plains.
Breeding grounds: Northern U.S. and Canada,
including Colorado.
Wintering grounds: Throughout U.S. and Mexico.
Comment: Almost always seen in large flocks,
roaming about in pursuit of insects and berries.
Often in residential areas.
Recommendation: Residential areas, Red Rocks
Park, Shadow Canyon; winter.

Shrikes
Northern Shrike
Dates in area: Winter resident and visitor; late
October to early April.
Local habitat: Foothills and plains; favors meadows
and semi-open grasslands.
Breeding grounds: Northern Canada and Alaska.
Comment: These northern hunters are fairly
common in our region during the colder months.
Feed primarily on small rodents.
Recommendation: Red Rocks Park, South Mesa
Trail, Green Mountain Trail; winter.

Loggerhead Shrike
Dates in area: Primarily April to October; smaller
   numbers in winter.
Local habitat: Semi-open country of foothills and
   plains.
Wintering grounds: Southern U.S. and Mexico.
Comment: Like the northern shrikes, usually seen
   alone, surveying hunting grounds from the top of
   a small tree or fencepost. Feed on insects, small
   birds and field mice.
Recommendation: Chatfield, Barr Lake; summer.

Vireos & Warblers
Solitary Vireo
Dates in area: Summer resident; May to October.
Local habitat: Conifer forests of mountains and
   foothills; woodlots on plains during migrations.

*The trees along Barr
Lake's eastern shore
attract a wide variety of
migrant songbirds.*

Wintering grounds: Coastal woodlands of southern U.S. and Central America.

Comment: Easily identified by the prominent white spectacles, these birds are common at times along forest trails. Fairly common on plains during migrations.

Recommendation: Gregory Canyon, May.

Warbling Vireo

Dates in area: Summer resident; May to September.

Local habitat: Wooded streams on plains and along ravines in lower foothills.

Wintering grounds: Central America.

Comment: Fairly common in the cottonwoods that line reservoirs and their feeder streams. Seem especially common during late summer, as their fall migration begins.

Recommendation: Chatfield, Barr Lake; September.

Orange-crowned Warbler

Dates in area: Summer resident; early May to mid-September.

Local habitat: Pinyon-Juniper Zone of the foothills.

Wintering grounds: Southern Texas and Mexico.

Comment: These warblers are most often found in the scrub-oak thickets that characterize the dry, lower foothills. Especially common during migrations.

Recommendation: South Mesa Trail, Mt. Falcon; mid-September.

Virginia's Warbler

Dates in area: Summer resident; May to early September.

Local habitat: Scrub-oak thickets along ravines of the lower foothills (Pinyon-Juniper Zone).

Wintering grounds: Central America.

Comment: Timid and easily overlooked. Feed and nest on or near the ground.

Recommendation: Red Rocks Park, Gregory
  Canyon; late May.

Yellow Warbler
Dates in area: Summer resident; May to September.
Local habitat: Thickets and small trees along
  streams and lake margins; wooded marshes;
  lower foothill canyons.
Wintering grounds: Central and South America.
Comment: Common in our region during the
  warmer months. Fairly common in residential
  areas, especially during migrations.
Recommendation: Highline Canal, Waterton
  Canyon; June.

Yellow-rumped Warbler
Dates in area: Summer resident; mid-April to early
  October.
Local habitat: Mountain forests during summer;
  woodlots on plains (including residential areas)
  during migrations.
Wintering grounds: Pacific coast and Mexico.
Comment: These warblers are abundant along
  streams and lake margins during migrations,
  especially in late April and late September. Arrive
  earlier and depart later than most other warblers.
Recommendation: Barr Lake, late April to early
  May; Mt. Evans area, summer.

Black-throated Gray Warbler
Dates in area: Summer resident; late April to
  September.
Local habitat: Sunny, dry slopes of the foothills
  (Pinyon-Juniper Zone).
Wintering grounds: Central America.
Comment: This warbler is usually found feeding
  among dry thickets on rocky, south-facing slopes
  of the foothill canyons.
Recommendation: Mt. Falcon, Waterton Canyon;
  September.

Yellowthroat
Dates in area: Summer resident; May to September.
Local habitat: Marshes, flooded woodlands.
Wintering grounds: Coastal areas of southern U.S.
and Mexico.
Comment: This small, noisy warbler is very
common in the marshes that border area reser-
voirs and streams.
Recommendation: Cherry Creek Reservoir, Sawhill
Ponds; summer.

Yellow-breasted Chat
Dates in area: Summer resident; May to September.
Local habitat: Thickets and shrubs along ravines of
the lower foothills.
Wintering grounds: South and Central America.
Comment: This large warbler is usually heard
before it is seen, noisily moving among the scrub-
oak thickets that border streams of the lower
foothills.
Recommendation: Red Rocks Park, Shadow
Canyon; June.

Ovenbird
Dates in area: Summer resident; May to September.
Local habitat: Moist undergrowth of foothill
forests.
Wintering grounds: Gulf Coast of southern U.S.
and Central America.
Comment: This ground-dwelling warbler is
inconspicuous and easily overlooked unless it
flushes as you move along the trail.
Recommendation: Gregory Canyon, Mt. Falcon,
Shadow Canyon; summer.

MacGillivray's Warbler
Dates in area: Summer resident; May to September.

Local habitat: Thickets along mountain streams during summer; along reservoirs and their feeder streams during migration.

Wintering grounds: Central America.

Comment: This bird favors moist thickets along ravines of the mountains and foothills, where it hunts for insects.

Recommendation: Waterton, Shadow and Gregory Canyons; summer.

Wilson's Warbler

Dates in area: Summer resident; May to early October.

Local habitat: Shrubs and thickets along streams, marshes and lakeshores; summer along high mountain lakes, up to timberline.

Wintering grounds: Central America.

Comment: Like MacGillivray's warbler, these birds feed on or near the ground. Fairly common around area reservoirs during migrations.

Recommendation: Mt. Evans area (especially Echo Lake), summer.

Starlings, Meadowlarks & Blackbirds

European Starling

Dates in area: All year.

Local habitat: Urban and rural areas on plains; especially abundant at feedlots.

Comment: These gregarious birds form huge flocks during the fall and winter months. Though they are considered to be a nuisance, they provide a tremendous service when it comes to insect control. Spotted winter plummage begins to appear by late August.

Recommendation: Chatfield, Barr Lake; late summer and fall.

Western Meadowlark

Dates in area: Primarily April to October; a few
    winter here.
Local habitat: Grasslands of plains and lower
    foothills.
Wintering grounds: Southern plains of U.S.
Comment: Perhaps the most conspicuous birds on
    western grasslands during the warmer months.
    Typically seen singing from fenceposts but often
    gather in large flocks, especially during late
    summer and fall.
Recommendation: Chatfield and Cherry Creek
    Recreation Areas; summer.

Yellow-headed Blackbird

Dates in area: Summer resident; April to early
    October.
Local habitat: Cattail marshes and adjacent grass-
    lands.
Wintering grounds: Southwestern U.S. and Central
    America.
Comment: These gregarious birds are common in
    our region during the warmer months but tend to
    localize at certain marshes and are not wide-
    spread.
Recommendation: West Quincy Lakes, Walden
    Ponds; May.

Red-winged Blackbird

Dates in area: All year; most abundant during
    warmer months.
Local habitat: Marshes and adjacent grasslands.
Comment: Thought to be the most abundant bird
    in the U.S. Form huge flocks during the colder
    months. Noisy flocks gather at area marshes
    during the summer.
Recommendation: Cherry Creek Reservoir,
    McClellan Reservoir; summer.

Brewer's Blackbird
Dates in area: Primarily a summer resident; April
   to October; small numbers may winter here.
Local habitat: Plains and mountain parklands.
Wintering grounds: Southern plains of U.S. and
   Mexico.
Comment: Though less common in our region than
   the other blackbirds included in this text, these
   birds are often seen in large flocks, especially
   during fall migration.
Recommendation: Barr Lake area; September and
   October.

Common Grackle
Dates in area: Primarily April to October; small
   number may remain through winter.
Local habitat: Fields, pastures, residential areas,
   urban parks.
Wintering grounds: Southern U.S.
Comment: These stately blackbirds are common in
   our region during the warmer months. Usually
   seen in small flocks, strutting across residential
   lawns or feeding in open fields. Gather in huge
   flocks by late summer.
Recommendation: Residential areas, summer.

Brown-headed Cowbird
Dates in area: Summer resident; April to September.
Local habitat: Fields, pastures, feedlots, farmlands.
Wintering grounds: Southern plains of U.S.
Comment: Fairly common on area grasslands
   during the warmer months. Usually seen in small
   flocks but often mingle with meadowlarks and
   other blackbirds. Seem especially common in
   thickets of lower foothills during the spring.
Recommendation: Red Rocks Park, Gregory
   Canyon; May and June.

Orioles & Tanagers

Northern Oriole (Bullock's Oriole)
Dates in area: Summer resident; May to September.
Local habitat: Woodlands and thickets along
  streams of the plains and lower foothills.
Wintering grounds: South America.
Comment: Bullock's oriole is the western counterpart of the Baltimore oriole. These noisy birds
  arrive in May to begin work on their hammock-
  like nests. Most abundant along ravines of the
  lower foothills, but also common along streams
  and lakes on the plains.
Recommendation: Red Rocks Park, Highline Canal,
  Barr Lake; June.

Western Tanager
Dates in area: Summer resident; May to September.
Local habitat: Open forests of foothills; woodlots
  on plains (especially along lakes) during
  migrations.
Wintering grounds: Central and South America.
Comment: These beautiful birds typically hunt for
  insects in the upper branches of the forest and
  are thus often overlooked. Most often seen on
  the plains during spring migration, when they
  visit residential areas. Usually alone or in pairs.
Recommendation: Chatfield Reservoir (south
  shore), mid-late May; Mt. Falcon Park, summer.

Grosbeaks, Finches & Crossbills

Black-headed Grosbeak
Dates in area: Summer resident; May to September.
Local habitat: Lower foothills (Pinyon-Juniper
  Zone).
Wintering grounds: Central and South America.
Comment: These large seed-eaters are usually seen

alone or in small flocks feeding on or near the
ground.
Recommendation: Red Rocks Park, late May
through June.

Evening Grosbeak
Dates in area: All year.
Local habitat: Higher mountain forests in summer;
descend to foothills and adjacent plains in winter.
Comment: Like red crossbills, these birds usually
move about in large flocks but their presence is
erratic and unpredictable. Occasionally turn up
at feeders in winter.
Recommendation: Green Mountain Trail,
November through February.

Blue Grosbeak
Dates in area: Summer resident; late May to early
September.
Local habitat: Open woodlands along streams and
lakeshores on plains.
Wintering grounds: Central and South America.
Comment: The male of this species is usually
encountered singing from the top of a small tree
or shrub. Generally found alone or in small,
scattered flocks.
Recommendation: Barr Lake, June through August.

Lazuli Bunting
Dates in area: Summer resident; May to September.
Local habitat: Marshy thickets and shrubs along
streams; especially common in lower foothills.
Wintering grounds: Central and South America.
Comment: These colorful birds are the western
counterpart of the indigo bunting. Like their
eastern relatives, they favor moist thickets near
streams and lakeshores.
Recommendation: Red Rocks Park, Shadow
Canyon; June.

Cassin's Finch
Dates in area: All year.
Local habitat: Mountain forests in summer;
  descend to foothills and adjacent plains in winter.
Comment: These finches are usually seen in small
  flocks, feeding on the ground with juncos.
  Occasionally seen with flocks of crossbills in the
  fall. Often turn up at feeders, especially in March
  and April.
Recommendation: South Mesa Trail, November.

House Finch
Dates in area: All year.
Local habitat: Residential areas, especially where
  large conifers are present. Also found in thickets
  along streams and marshes.
Comment: These small finches are very common in
  the Denver-Boulder suburbs throughout the year.
  Abundant at feeders during the colder months.
Recommendation: Backyard feeders, November to
  May; Cherry Creek marsh, summer.

Pine Grosbeak
Dates in area: All year.
Local habitat: Mountain forests (especially along
  meadows) in summer; descend to open foothill
  forests in winter.
Comment: These large finches are usually found
  alone or in pairs during the summer. Gather in
  small flocks during the colder months, when they
  are fairly common in the open ponderosa woodlands of the Transition Zone.
Recommendation: Green Mountain Trail, November through February.

Rosy Finches
Dates in area: Brown-capped—all year. Gray-
  crowned and black—November to early March.
Local habitat: Tundra and open timberline wood-

lands in summer; rocky slopes, canyons and other open areas of mountains and foothills during winter.

Breeding grounds: Brown-capped—alpine areas of local mountains. Gray-crowned—Pacific Northwest. Black—northern Rockies.

Comment: Usually feed and move about in large flocks. Most often seen on ground, feeding along snowbanks and alpine lakes.

Recommendation: Brown-capped—Mt. Evans (especially around Summit Lake), July. Gray-crowned and black—Squaw Pass Road, November.

Open forest near the summit of Guanella Pass is a good place to find pine grosbeaks and Cassin's finches.

Common Redpoll
Dates in area: Winter resident and visitor; late
    November to March.
Local habitat: Weedy thickets at margin of wood-
    lots, fields, and marshes on plains.
Breeding grounds: Alaska and Northern Canada.
Comment: These small finches are usually found in
    thickets, feeding with winter sparrows. Their
    numbers vary greatly from year to year.
Recommendation: Barr Lake, winter.

Pine Siskin
Dates in area: All year.
Local habitat: Mountain forests in summer; foot-
    hills and wooded areas on plains during winter.
Comment: These birds are common at backyard
    feeders during late winter and early spring, where
    they mingle with house finches. Their ascending
    call heralds their presence.
Recommendation: Mt. Falcon, September; back-
    yard feeders, April.

American Goldfinch
Dates in area: All year but most common late April
    to late October.
Local habitat: Thickets and shrubs along fields,
    marshes and streams of plains and lower foothills.
Comment: These colorful birds are most con-
    spicuous in the late spring and early summer,
    when they often move about in large flocks.
    Fairly common in residential areas during spring
    migration.
Recommendation: Cherry Creek Marsh, summer;
    Lower Waterton Canyon, June.

Lesser Goldfinch
Dates in area: Summer resident; late May to early
    October.

Local habitat: Open ponderosa pine forests of the foothills.
Wintering grounds: Southwestern U.S.
Comment: These small finches favor the dry, sunny areas of the foothills, where open stands of ponderosa pine finger their way into the Pinyon-Juniper Zone.
Recommendation: Waterton Canyon, Gregory Canyon; summer.

Red Crossbill
Dates in area: All year.
Local habitat: Mountain forests in the summer; descend to foothill forests during colder months; may wander onto plains in late winter.
Comment: These erratic wanderers are usually seen in large flocks. Often feed with evening grosbeaks, mountain chickadees and Cassin's finches. The sound of a flock "attacking" a pine tree resembles a crackling fire.
Recommendation: South Mesa Trail, Green Mountain Trail; November.

Towhees

Green-tailed Towhee
Dates in area: Summer resident; May to early October.
Local habitat: Lower foothills (Pinyon-Juniper Zone).
Wintering grounds: Arizona and Mexico.
Comment: These attractive birds are usually found in small, scattered flocks, feeding on the ground on dry, rocky slopes of the lower foothills. They will often appear from under a patch of scrub oak, walking ahead of you as you hike along the trail.
Recommendation: South Mesa Trail, Gregory Canyon, Mt. Falcon; summer.

Towhees are abundant along South Mesa Trail.

Rufous-sided Towhee
Dates in area: All year but much more common during the warmer months.
Local habitat: Pinyon-Juniper Zone, especially in scrub-oak thickets along ravines of the lower foothills.
Comment: These flashy birds are common, noisy residents of the lower foothills. Usually found alone, scratching away under a shrub, searching for seeds and insects. Fairly common in residential areas, especially during migration.
Recommendation: Red Rocks Park, South Mesa Trail; summer.

Sparrows, Juncos & Longspurs
House Sparrow
Dates in area: All year.

Local habitat: Wide variety of habitats throughout both urban and rural areas.

Comment: This well-known and abundant bird is usually found in small flocks along curbs, alleys and weedy fields; also common around silos and feedlots.

Recommendation: Residential areas, all year.

Savannah Sparrow

Dates in area: Summer resident; mid-April to mid-October.

Local habitat: Short grass prairie, foothill grasslands, mountain meadows; tundra in late summer.

Wintering grounds: Southern U.S. and Mexico.

Comment: Though they may be seen in large flocks during fall migration, these ground dwellers are more often seen in small scattered flocks, feeding on open grasslands. When surprised on the trail they usually dart into the dense vegetation rather than fly off.

Recommendation: South Mesa Trail, late summer.

Lark Bunting

Dates in area: Summer resident; May to September.

Local habitat: Prairie grasslands.

Wintering grounds: Texas and Mexico.

Comment: Colorado's State Bird. Usually seen in large flocks, feeding on open grasslands.

Recommendation: Barr Lake area (especially along Tower Road), summer.

Vesper Sparrow

Dates in area: Summer resident; April to mid-October.

Local habitat: Open grasslands of foothills and plains.

Wintering grounds: Southern U.S. and Mexico.

Comment: Usually found in small scattered flocks, feeding along trails and unpaved roads. Often sing from fences and rock formations.

Recommendation: Red Rocks Park, South Mesa
Trail; summer.

Lark Sparrow
Dates in area: Summer resident; May to September.
Local habitat: Grasslands of foothills and plains.
Wintering grounds: Southwestern U.S. and
    Mexico.
Comment: These distinctive sparrows are often
    abundant on area grasslands during the summer
    months; especially common along the base of the
    foothills.
Recommendation: Red Rocks Park, South Mesa
    Trail; summer.

Dark-eyed Juncos
Dates in area: Gray-headed—all year. Slate-colored,
    Oregon, white-winged—October to April.
Local habitat: Gray-headeds inhabit rocky clearings
    in forest from foothills to tundra during warmer
    months; descend to foothill canyons and onto
    plains in winter. Others are found in brushy
    areas on plains and in foothills, especially in
    open stands of conifers. White-winged race tends
    to stay in the foothills.
Breeding grounds: Slate-colored—Canada and
    Alaska. Oregon—Pacific Northwest. White-
    winged—Black Hills of South Dakota.
Comment: Juncos are usually found in large, mixed
    flocks, often feeding with Cassin's finches or tree
    sparrows. Slate-colored and Oregon races are
    fairly common at urban backyard feeders, es-
    pecially in March and April.
Recommendation: Gray-headed—Mt. Evans area,
    Mt. Falcon; summer. All four—South Mesa
    Trail/Shadow Canyon, Red Rocks Park; winter.

Tree Sparrow
Dates in area: Winter resident; late October to
    March.

Local habitat: Thickets along marshes, streams and
woodlots on plains.
Breeding grounds: Northern Canada and Alaska.
Comment: These winter sparrows are abundant
around area lakes and marshes during the colder
months. Almost always found in large, scattered
flocks.
Recommendation: Sawhill Ponds, Barr Lake; winter.

Chipping Sparrow
Dates in area: Summer resident; late April to
October.
Local habitat: Favor ponderosa pine forests of
Transition Zone. Common in woodlots on plains
during migrations.
Wintering grounds: Southern U.S. and Mexico.
Comment: These sparrows are especially common
on the plains during early May, when their
spring migration peaks. During the summer look
for them along meadows in the foothills.
Recommendation: Mt. Falcon, Upper Gregory
Canyon, Green Mountain; summer.

Brewer's Sparrow
Dates in area: Summer resident; late April to late
September.
Local habitat: Dry scrub-grassland, especially along
the base of the foothills.
Wintering grounds: Southwestern U.S. and
Mexico.
Comment: This plain sparrow is fairly common on
the dry lower-foothill grasslands during the
warmer months. Most abundant during migra-
tions in early May and late September.
Recommendation: South Mesa Trail, September.

Clay-colored Sparrow
Dates in area: Summer resident; mid-April to early
October.

Local habitat: Dry thickets along ravines of the lower foothills; adjacent foothill grasslands.

Wintering grounds: Southern Texas and Mexico.

Comment: Very similar in appearance and habitat to the Brewer's sparrow. Most common during fall migration, especially in the scrub-oak thickets that blanket the Pinyon-Juniper Zone.

Recommendation: South Mesa Trail, late September to early October.

White-crowned Sparrow

Dates in area: Primarily mid-April through October; small numbers may linger through the winter.

Local habitat: Nest along alpine lakes, especially near timberline. Common in thickets along foothill ravines, streams and lakes during migrations.

Wintering grounds: Southern U.S. and Mexico.

Comment: Migrations across plains peak in early May and early October.

Recommendation: Barr Lake, early May; Mt. Evans, summer; South Mesa Trail, late September.

Lincoln's Sparrow

Dates in area: Summer resident; May to early October.

Local habitat: Summer in mountain meadows, especially along streams and alpine lakes; migrant on plains.

Wintering grounds: Southwestern U.S. and Mexico.

Comment: These inconspicuous sparrows favor marshy areas along mountain streams and alpine lakes. Fairly common along lower foothills during migrations.

Recommendation: Echo Lake, summer; South Mesa Trail, late September.

Song Sparrow

Dates in area: All year.

Local habitat: Favor thickets along streams,
  marshes and lakes of the plains and lower
  foothills.
Comment: Common in our region throughout the
  year. However, since they favor dense thickets,
  they are more often heard than seen.
Recommendation: Chatfield (especially Plum
  Creek), Cherry Creek Reservoir; April and May.

Longspurs
Dates in area: McCown's and chestnut-collared—
  all year. Lapland—November to March.
Local habitat: Short-grass prairie.
Comment: All three species are irregular and
  uncommon visitors in our region. When present,
  they are usually seen in large flocks. Often found
  feeding with horned larks and grassland sparrows.
Recommendation: Barr Lake and surrounding
  countryside, winter.

Ring-necked Pheasant.

Recommended Field Trips

A visit to any of the birding areas covered in this text will be enjoyable and interesting at any time of the year. The following trips are suggested with four goals in mind.

To expose the birder to a wide variety of birds and other wildlife.

To direct the birder to "major events" that occur throughout the year such as migrations, territorial displays, mating behavior, etc.

To encourage the birder to visit the various bird habitats during the different seasons, thereby illustrating the effects of climate, water supply and food crop on the local bird populations.

To assist the birder by organizing and condensing information that is presented in the other sections of this text.

SPRING March

Early March
Place: Mt. Falcon.
Highlights: Prairie falcons, Steller's jays, hairy woodpeckers, mountain chickadees, pygmy and white-breasted nuthatches, crows, Abert's squirrels.

Mid-March
Place: Sawhill/Walden Ponds.
Highlights: American widgeons, mallards, gadwalls, green-winged teal, shovelers, redheads, ring-necked ducks, Canada geese, coot, tree and song sparrows, muskrats.

Late March
Place: West Quincy Lakes.
Highlights: Pied-billed grebes, gadwalls, canvas-backs, redheads, lesser scaup, common golden-eyes, buffleheads.

April

Early April
Place: McClellan Reservoir.
Highlights: Possible loons (common and arctic), horned grebes, western grebes, lesser scaup, common mergansers, hooded mergansers, common goldeneyes.

Mid-April
Place: Green Mountain Trail.
Highlights: Cooper's hawks, sharp-shinned hawks, turkey vultures, territorial display of resident woodpeckers (northern flickers, hairy woodpeckers and Williamson's sapsuckers), mountain chickadees, white-breasted and pygmy nut-

hatches, Steller's jays, common ravens, Townsend's solitaires, mountain and western bluebirds,
red crossbills, gray-headed juncos.

Late April
Place: Cherry Creek Reservoir.
Highlights: Western grebes, horned grebes, blue-
winged teal, shovelers, kestrels, northern harriers,
possible white-faced ibis, common snipe, ring-
billed gulls, killdeer, ring-necked pheasants,
western meadowlarks, mourning doves, magpies,
American goldfinches, jackrabbits.

May
Early May
Place: Barr Lake.
Highlights: Western grebes (good time to see
mating dance), blue-winged and cinnamon teal,
shovelers, Swainson's hawks, white pelicans,
double-crested cormorants, possible white-faced
ibis, Wilson's phalaropes, spotted sandpipers,
tree swallows, eastern and western kingbirds,
western wood pewees, Swainson's thrushes,
house wrens, yellow-rumped warblers, white-
crowned and chipping sparrows, red foxes (possi-
bly with cubs).

Mid-May
Place: Gregory Canyon.
Highlights: Cooper's hawks, turkey vultures,
Steller's jays, canyon wrens, brown-headed cow-
birds, solitary vireos, western wood pewees,
Virginia's warblers, pine siskins, rufous-sided
towhees, rock squirrels, red squirrels.

Place: Chatfield Reservoir.
Highlights: Western grebes, blue-winged and cinnamon teal, wood ducks, kestrels, great blue

herons, double-crested cormorants, shorebirds (including avocets, stilt sandpipers, black-bellied plovers), burrowing owls, great horned owls, belted kingfishers, barn and tree swallows, eastern kingbirds, house wrens, western meadowlarks, western tanagers, yellow warblers, American goldfinches, song sparrows, thirteen-lined ground squirrels, prairie dogs.

Late May
Place: Red Rocks Park.
Highlights: Scrub jays, common poor-wills (evening), northern orioles, brown-headed cowbirds, white-throated swifts, barn and violet-green swallows, Say's phoebes, Virginia's warblers, yellow warblers, yellow-breasted chats, black-headed grosbeaks, lazuli buntings, rufous-sided towhees, rock squirrels.

SUMMER June

Early June
Place: South Mesa Trail/Shadow Canyon Trail.
Highlights: Red-tailed and Swainson's hawks, prairie falcons, kestrels, Steller's jays, Townsend's solitaires, MacGillivray's warblers, yellow-breasted chats, rock and canyon wrens, western meadowlarks, green-tailed and rufous-sided towhees, lesser goldfinches, lazuli buntings, black-headed grosbeaks, yellow-bellied marmots, mule deer.

Mid-June
Place: Waterton Canyon.
Highlights: Turkey vultures, golden eagles, kestrels, belted kingfishers, swallows (barn, cliff, violet-green), white-throated swifts, rock and canyon wrens, possible yellow-billed cuckoos, gray cat-

birds, yellow warblers, MacGillivray's warblers, lesser goldfinches, lazuli buntings, bighorn sheep, mule deer, rock squirrels.

Late June
Place: Mt. Falcon Park.

Highlights: Cooper's and sharp-shinned hawks, prairie falcons, merlins, Steller's jays, scrub jays, mountain chickadees, nuthatches (all three), rufous-sided and green-tailed towhees, western tanagers, yellow warblers, western bluebirds, black-headed grosbeaks, gray-headed juncos, chipping sparrows, Abert's squirrels, rock squirrels, chipmunks.

July
Early July
Place: Mt. Evans area.

Highlights: Possible white-tailed ptarmigan, possible blue grouse, northern goshawks, common ravens, yellow-bellied sapsuckers, three-toed woodpeckers, mountain bluebirds, water pipits, olive-sided and Hammond's flycatchers, gray jays, Clarke's nutcrackers, Townsend's solitaires, ruby-crowned and golden-crowned kinglets, hermit thrushes, possible veeries, Wilson's warblers, Cassin's finches, brown-capped rosy finches, white-crowned and Lincoln's sparrows, alpine wildflowers, pikas, golden-mantled ground squirrels, red squirrels, yellow-bellied marmots, mountain goats, bighorn sheep, possible elk.

Mid-July
Place: Chatfield Reservoir.

Highlights: Mallards with young, wood ducks with young, great blue herons, cormorants, American bitterns, belted kingfishers, eastern and western kingbirds, great horned owls, northern orioles, western meadowlarks, burrowing owls, barn and tree swallows, warbling vireos, yellowthroats, lazuli buntings, lark sparrows, beavers, muskrats.

Late July
Place: Gregory Canyon.
Highlights: Cooper's hawks, merlins, turkey vultures, rock and canyon wrens, broad-tailed hummingbirds, solitary vireos, western wood pewees, western and dusky flycatchers, MacGillivray's and Virginia's warblers, green-tailed towhees, lesser goldfinches, chipping sparrows, red squirrels, rock squirrels, yellow-bellied marmots, chipmunks.

August

Early August
Place: Barr Lake.
Highlights: Western grebes with young, white pelicans, red-tailed hawks, ferruginous hawks, snowy egrets, Franklin's and California gulls, early shorebirds (long-billed curlews, marbled godwits, stilt sandpipers, western and semipalmated sandpipers), red-headed woodpeckers, eastern and western kingbirds, possible yellow-billed cuckoos, lark buntings, blue grosbeaks.

Mid-August
Place: Sawhill/Walden Ponds.
Highlights: Red-tailed hawks, kestrels, black-crowned night herons, green-backed herons, soras, Virginia rails, American bitterns, killdeer, spotted sandpipers, great horned owls, rough-winged swallows, yellow-headed blackbirds, marsh wrens, eastern kingbirds, yellowthroats, American goldfinches, song sparrows, muskrats, beavers.

Late August
Place: Green Mountain Trail
Highlights: Cooper's and sharp-shinned hawks, possible blue grouse, violet-green swallows, mountain and western bluebirds, olive-sided flycatchers, western wood pewees, Steller's jays, Townsend's solitaires, Williamson's sapsuckers, hairy woodpeckers, pine siskins, chipping sparrows.

September   FALL

Early September
Place: Barr Lake.
Highlights: Western grebes, eared grebes, pied-billed grebes, white pelicans, snowy egrets, possible cattle egrets, black terns, Forster's terns, California and Franklin's gulls, peak shorebird migration (including Baird's sandpipers, least sandpipers, sanderlings, avocets, black-bellied plovers, solitary sandpipers), Wilson's and northern phalaropes, lark buntings, vesper and lark sparrows, savannah sparrows, mule and white-tailed deer.

Mid-September
Place: Mt. Falcon Park.
Highlights: Cooper's and sharp-shinned hawks, prairie falcons, merlins, turkey vultures, blue grouse, wild turkeys, band-tailed pigeons, hairy woodpeckers, Steller's jays, western and mountain bluebirds, warblers (yellow-rumped, black-throated gray, orange-crowned), Townsend's solitaries, pine siskins, Abert's squirrels, possible bobcats, mule deer.

Late September
Place: South Mesa Trail / Shadow Canyon Trail.

Highlights: Red-tailed hawks, prairie falcons, merlins, rock wrens, mountain chickadees, nuthatches (all three), Steller's jays, Wilson's and orange-crowned warblers, rufous-sided and green-tailed towhees, vesper sparrows, lark sparrows, savannah sparrows, white-crowned and clay-colored sparrows, mule deer.

October

Early October
Place: Chatfield Reservoir.
Highlights: Western and pied-billed grebes, American widgeons, coot, possible ospreys, northern harriers, great horned owls, burrowing owls, Wilson's and northern phalaropes, black-billed magpies, migrant sparrows (chipping, Lincoln's, white-crowned).

Mid-October.
Place: Sawhill/Walden Ponds.
Highlights: Pied-billed grebes, pintail, gadwalls, widgeons, green-winged teal, ring-necked ducks, possible greater white-fronted geese, possible ospreys, common snipe, yellowlegs.

Late October
Place: Barr Lake.
Highlights: Common loons, possible arctic loons, horned grebes, northern shovelers, green-winged teal, ruddy ducks, buffleheads, Canada geese, red-tailed hawks, northern harriers, possible peregrine falcons, ring-billed and Franklin's gulls, sandhill cranes, yellowlegs, long-billed dowitchers, tree sparrows.

November

Early November
Place: South Mesa Trail.

Highlights: Red-tailed hawks, rough-legged hawks,
  downy and hairy woodpeckers, canyon wrens,
  mountain chickadees, nuthatches (all three),
  brown creepers, Townsend's solitaires, red crossbills, Cassin's finches, dark-eyed juncos (all four;
  good place to see white-winged species), mule
  deer.

Place: West Quincy Lakes.
Highlights: American widgeons, gadwalls, redheads, lesser scaup, buffleheads, common goldeneyes, coot, Canada geese.

Mid-November
Place: Waterton Canyon.
Highlights: Red-tailed hawks, golden eagles,
  kestrels, scrub jays, possible Lewis' woodpeckers,
  canyon wrens, dippers, Townsend's solitaires,
  dark-eyed juncos, bighorn sheep (rutting season).

Late November
Place: Cherry Creek Reservoir.
Highlights: Common loons, common goldeneyes,
  hooded and common mergansers, Canada geese,
  ring-necked pheasants, ring-billed gulls, great
  horned owls, horned larks, song sparrows.

December

WINTER

Early December
Place: Gregory Canyon.
Highlights: Steller's jays, common ravens, canyon
  wrens, possible saw-whet and pygmy owls, nuthatches, black-capped and mountain chickadees,
  Townsend's solitaires, possible evening and pine
  grosbeaks, dark-eyed juncos.

Mid-December
Place: McClellan Reservoir.

Highlights: Common goldeneyes, buffleheads, common and hooded mergansers, lesser scaup, possible canvasbacks, ring-billed gulls, herring gulls, coot.

Late December
Place: Barr Lake.
Highlights: Wintering ducks, Canada geese, rough-legged hawks, kestrels, bald eagles, great horned and screech owls, possible long-eared owls, downy woodpeckers, northern shrikes, horned larks, common redpolls, tree sparrows, possible longspurs.

January
Early January
Place: Red Rocks Park.
Highlights: Rock doves, magpies, scrub jays, northern shrikes, wintering robins, Townsend's solitaires, black-capped chickadees, dark-eyed juncos, possible rosy finches.

Mid-January
Place: Green Mountain Trail.
Highlights: Possible northern goshawks, hairy woodpeckers, northern shrikes, common ravens, white-breasted and pygmy nuthatches, brown creepers, mountain chickadees, pine grosbeaks, possible evening grosbeaks and red crossbills, mule deer.

Late January
Place: Mt. Evans area.
Highlights: Northern goshawks, gray jays, Clarke's nutcrackers, common ravens, white-breasted nut-hatches, mountain chickadees, golden-crowned kinglets, possible pygmy owls, three-toed wood-

peckers, hairy woodpeckers, possible rosy finches, red squirrels.

February

Early February
Place: Chatfield Reservoir
Highlights: Red-tailed hawks, rough-legged hawks, kestrels, belted kingfishers, great horned owls, downy woodpeckers, possible Lewis' woodpeckers, brown creepers, white-breasted and red-breasted nuthatches, northern shrikes, horned larks, possible longspurs, common redpolls, tree sparrows, dark-eyed juncos.

Mid-February
Place: Guanella Pass.
Highlights: Northern goshawks, common ravens, white-tailed ptarmigan, gray jays, Clarke's nutcrackers, mountain chickadees, golden-crowned kinglets, possible rosy finches.

Late February
Place: Barr Lake.
Highlights: Northern pintail, mallards, green-winged teal, common mergansers, rough-legged hawks, possible bald eagles, kestrels, great horned owls, screech owls, horned larks, northern shrikes, downy woodpeckers, black-capped chickadees, American goldfinches, common redpolls, possible longspurs, mule deer, red foxes.

Bibliography

Bailey, Alfred M. and Robert J. Niedrach, *Pictorial Checklist of Colorado Birds*, Denver Museum of Natural History, 1967

Bull, John and John Farrand, Jr., *The Audubon Society Field Guide to North American Birds, Eastern Region*, The American Museum of Natural History, Alfred A. Knopf, Inc., New York, 1977

Lechleitner, R. R., *Wild Mammals of Colorado*, Pruett Publishing Co., Boulder, 1969

Niedrach, Robert J. and Robert B. Rockwell, *The Birds of Denver and Mountain Parks*, Denver Museum of Natural History, 1939 (revised 1959)

Palmer, E. Laurence and H. Seymour Fowler, *Fieldbook of Natural History*, Second Edition, McGraw-Hill, Inc., 1975

Peterson, Roger Tory, *A Field Guide to the Birds, East of the Rockies*, Houghton Mifflin Company, Boston, 1980

Robbins, Chandler S., Bertel Bruun and Herbert S. Zim, *A Guide to Field Identification, Birds of North America*, Golden Press, Western Publishing Co., Inc., New York, 1966

Index